Advance Praise for *The Practical Marketer*

"Saurabh's mix of keen insights and practical knowledge of the field of marketing makes *The Practical Marketer* a practical certainty for those in their formative years in marketing. A must read, and a must keep for all aspiring marketers."

— **Bharat Puri**, Managing Director, Pidilite Industries

"*The Practical Marketer* is written keeping the consumer product marketer in mind. It delves into every aspect of marketing, including consumer understanding, branding, go-to-market strategies, and more. Filled with examples and cases, this book is a treasure trove of information and practical knowledge. The author, Saurabh Bajaj, has packed his 20 years of consumer brand marketing wisdom into this handy book. A veritable treasure trove of ideas and tips."

— **Ambi Parameswaran**, Veteran Adman, Bestselling Author, Brand Coach

"Saurabh has penned together a much-needed practical, step-by-step guide to marketing. Built on his personal experience and insights, replete with real-life examples. A must read if you are an aspiring marketer."

— **Anand Kripalu**, MD and Global CEO, Blackstone-backed EPL; former MD at Diageo India and President Asia, Mondelez (Cadbury)

"Saurabh Bajaj's *The Practical Marketer* offers actionable advice and real-world examples for navigating modern marketing challenges effectively."

—**Varun Berry,** Executive Vice Chairman and MD, Britannia Industries

"Saurabh's two decades as a practical marketer and his accumulation of real-world experiences and insights across multiple categories and brands gets captured succinctly in this narrative that he puts out to inspire young minds. Needless to say, his passion to impart knowledge in an easy and comprehensive fashion makes it an extremely handy read for aspiring marketers."

—**Avneesh Khosla,** Chief Marketing Officer, Vodafone Idea Ltd.

"*The Practical Marketer* by Saurabh Bajaj is a great entry to consumers, brands, and marketing. Through his irrepressible and layman style, he has democratized marketing through simplified concepts brought alive by real life examples and situations. Great way to explore the world of marketing…. A must read!"

—**Gunjan Shah,** MD and CEO, Bata India Limited.

As the name suggests, Saurabh's book is a treasure trove of practical insights for anyone who wants to make a career in marketing. It will be of great value to both students as well as marketing professionals.

—**Nitin Saini,** Vice President Marketing, Mondelez

"Most marketing books teach you what marketing is all about—its concepts and principles. This one goes a step beyond and tells you how to be a good marketer—the processes and tools that you can use to arrive at a sound marketing strategy and plan. A truly invaluable resource for anybody in marketing or aspiring to get there."

—**Rohit Srivastava,** Chief Strategy Officer, Contract Advertising, India

"Saurabh's *The Practical Marketer* is a great encyclopedia for students of marketing and young marketing professionals. It's a practical Kotler of our times for marketing in the complex Indian stage. In the fast-paced world today, the traditional mentoring and learning on the job is losing its sheen. In other cases, brand managers find it awkward to ask basic questions on-the-go during everyday work. *The Practical Marketer* can be a ready reckoner for all those times."

—**Nikhil Rao,** CMO Mars Wrigley, India

"Saurabh's passion for teaching marketing to young budding marketers comes through. A must-read set of checklists, tick boxes, and examples for aspiring marketing students."

—**Vinay Subramanyam,** Senior Director, Marketing, Kellanova, India

"In a country where most MBAs do the course without much practical experience, they can feel quite clueless in their early years. This book bridges the gap and is a great guide to learning the tricks and trade of the job called marketing.

Saurabh expertly draws from his wide experience and observations of brands across multiple industries and creates a structured and categorized mental diagram of what young marketers should expect, and how they can contribute to their jobs and build their careers."

—**Ganapathy Balagopalan,**
Deputy Chief Strategy Officer, Ogilvy India

"Right from when Saurabh was a young marketer in Cadbury during the early 2010s, his voice would be heard in the meetings involving the ace Cadbury marketing stalwarts and Contract Advertising. Never shy, always clear, always objective and fearless, one knew that his was a voice that would shine. Which is now even more amply reflected in *The Practical Marketer* where he shares the fundamentals of marketing for young hopefuls. A must read for youngsters coming into the marketing universe."

—**Raj Nair,** Growth and Creative Consultant.
Former CEO and CCO, Madison BMB

"Practicality overrides everything. Saurabh's efforts attempt to bridge the chasm between lofty, world-changing pursuits by industry authors who are busy building their personal brands and academia resorting to creating theoretical comprehensibility and intelligence to offset their poor awareness of cutting-edge, real-world developments. Quite like him, his book is a sincere and an essential guide well aligned with the modern marketer's job descriptions."

—**Ashish Mishra,** CEO, Interbrand India & South Asia

THE PRACTICAL MARKETER

YOUR ULTIMATE GUIDE TO CONSUMER PRODUCT MARKETING

SAURABH BAJAJ

JAICO PUBLISHING HOUSE

Ahmedabad Bangalore Chennai
Delhi Hyderabad Kolkata Mumbai

Published by Jaico Publishing House
A-2 Jash Chambers, 7-A Sir Phirozshah Mehta Road
Fort, Mumbai - 400 001
jaicopub@jaicobooks.com
www.jaicobooks.com

To be sold only in India, Bangladesh, Bhutan,
Pakistan, Nepal, Sri Lanka and the Maldives.

THE PRACTICAL MARKETER
ISBN 978-81-19792-16-0

First Jaico Impression: 2024
Second Jaico Impression: 2024

Page design and layout by Jojy Philip, Delhi

CONTENTS

CONTENTS

Dedicated to my sons,
Krishay and Taanish

PREFACE

While growing up, I was fascinated by pure sciences and initially dreamt of becoming a physicist. However, like many students with similar aspirations, I instead qualified for a course in civil engineering at Delhi College of Engineering. During a train ride from Mumbai to Delhi, I met a few MBA students who were pursuing their management studies from the Indian Institute of Management, Mumbai (formerly known as NITIE Mumbai) and the topics they discussed fascinated me. This chance encounter eventually paved the way for me to discover my passion for marketing.

Post my engineering, I joined IIM Indore in 2002 and was elected as the Secretary of Mercur-I, the marketing club at IIM Indore. As a student, I went on to establish Utsaha—Institute's annual marketing research fest—along with my batchmates. My curiosity for brand management was further fuelled during my summer internship with The Coca Cola Company where I observed how a campaign like *'Thanda Matlab Coca Cola'* can turbocharge an entire brand category and bring about a sea change in consumer behaviour. I then went on to work with Mondelez India on several iconic campaigns, including Cadbury Celebrations (*'Toh Iss Diwali Aap Kise Khush Karange'*), Cadbury Gems (*'Raho Umarless'*), and more recently Britannia Cheese StarChef, a 12-part YouTube series starring Saif Ali Khan. I also worked extensively in sales, innovation, and international business, learning the nuances of different functions.

As I rose to the position of marketing head with Britannia's Dairy category, I realized that at 40 I have had an eventful career and wondered about my next move. Eventually, during this phase of contemplation, a few things happened at once: a stroll with my wife, where she nudged me to channelize my energy into exploring further options; a close friend, Kalyan Challapalli, urged me to seek avenues to share my knowledge; and the penny dropped when Gautam Gupta, a close mentor and guide, planted a seed of thought in my mind that 40 is the right age to shift one's attitude from an achievement orientation to a contribution orientation. It's important then to understand how one can make a difference in others' lives and not just chase more achievements for oneself.

Taking this advice to heart, I began writing articles and posts on LinkedIn and realized that there exists a wide gulf between theoretical aspects of marketing as taught in schools and colleges and the way it is actually practised. This led to the creation of the book that you hold in your hands *The Practical Marketer*. This book serves as a practitioner's guide to marketing which is followed in companies that manufacture consumer products. If you are a student, an early jobber in sales wanting to move on to marketing, a brand manager who has just started his or her journey, or an entrepreneur, you may even be a person who is only peripherally aware of the field of marketing and wonder what the inner workings of this field are, then this book is for you.

The book doesn't assume any prior knowledge of marketing. It simplifies concepts with minimal jargon and is rich with my personal experiences as a marketer and recent campaigns I managed to spearhead, so that you can relate to what is written and gain an in-depth understanding from a practitioner's perspective.

1

ESSENTIALS OF BRAND STRATEGY

Basics of Brand Management

Building a Category Strategy

How Is a Brand Strategy Built?

Crafting a Brand Purpose

BASICS OF BRAND MANAGEMENT

In 2004, I graduated from IIM Indore and took up a job with Wipro Consumer Care & Lightning Group in Uttarakhand where I learned to push sales for brands like Santoor, Milk & Roses (soap), Wipro Active Talc, and so on. These brands had a little market presence and it was a challenging job as one had to convince every individual retailer about the brand and its benefits. However, when I joined Mondelez India's celebrated brand Cadbury as the Area Sales Manager in Vijayawada, I could feel the power of selling an established brand that is already a market leader. The respect that one receives from the market and the openness for new innovations makes the task much easier. All these experiences helped me realize that the levers that a brand marketer deploys can directly impact a brand's offtakes in a meaningful manner.

In 2008, I was promoted as the brand manager for Cadbury Dairy Milk and Gems and began working at the head office in Mumbai and subsequently went on to manage Cadbury Celebrations. However, as I moved from sales to marketing, a few questions arose in my mind:

- What is the difference between sales and marketing?
- How do I assess how well I'm doing?
- What exactly are my day-to-day responsibilities?
- What data am I supposed to be familiar with?
- How do I create or develop a brand vision?

Let's now explore answers to some of these questions.

Sales vs. Marketing

> While a salesperson's job is to make sure that the stock is always within the reach of the customer, a marketer's job is to increase brand offtakes, which is the actual movement of the product off the shelf.

In this regard, a salesperson considers additional avenues for increasing sell-in, whereas a marketer is often concerned with retail sell-outs. A sales manager is obsessed with data cuts and gaps that could be filled. Their typical day at work would be to keep an eye on any opportunity to maximize business through the right channel (modern or traditional trade), geography (tier-1 towns, tier-2 towns, and so on), brand, or Stock Keeping Unit (SKUs, also known as pack sizes), and supervise the team members who may be reporting to them.

However, when it comes to marketing, the variables shift dramatically. A marketer should consider product opportunities (launching new flavours or variants), pricing opportunities (launching new SKUs), channel opportunities (hiring visibility in modern trade or e-commerce), and activation opportunities (advertising or consumer promotions).

While company and market share growth are ultimately measured by both sales and marketing, the portions of the mix that they focus on frequently complement each other. For instance, the key task of growing distribution usually lies with a salesperson, whereas driving numeric distribution by introducing affordable price point and spreading awareness by approaching the relevant media is driven by the marketing team. In another example, the task of a sales team is measured based on the business delivery, however, the key levers to enable the same through advertising, promotions, and innovations are usually operated by a marketing team.

Hence, in a successful organization, both the sales and marketing functions collaborate to deliver business objectives.

Brand Responsibilities

All of us have heard of the four Ps of marketing–product, price, place, and promotion. The way these elements break down into brand tasks is as follows:

1. **Brand strategy:** This includes understanding the consumer proposition that the brand owns and how it stands out from its competition. Implications of these would be found in advertising, activation, and promotions. These topics will be covered in subsequent sections.

2. **Channel strategy:** This includes building the right business growth strategy across a host of channels such as modern trade, traditional trade, geographical regions, and so on. The levers that the brand manager holds could include activation and visibility budgets.

3. **Artwork management:** This is one of the most crucial but also tiresome responsibilities of a brand manager where one is expected to coordinate between the chosen art agency (with the copywriters, artwork designers, etc.) and the legal and regulatory departments of the company before the artwork goes to print.

4. **Product innovation or managing cross-functional team:** This is the second part of the job responsibility that is time-consuming. This includes initiating a project to ensure each functional team is held accountable from delivery till the product reaches the market.

5. **Product recipe:** All brands have a product recipe which remains fixed, however, product packaging may change as per the changes mentioned in packaging and labeling regulations.

6. **Price increases:** These are usually governed by commodity prices and the alarm for the same is usually raised by the finance team. Often, this is a bitter pill to swallow, but it's equally crucial to manage the brands profitability. This is often assessed by the number of performance metrics.

7. **SKU strategy:** A brand typically has a number of SKUs (pack sizes) of various grammages (for e.g., 100g, 50g, etc.) and MRPs (for e.g., ₹5, ₹10, ₹15, ₹20, and so on) managing the performance of each variant. Eliminating some SKUs and adding others is another portion of the mix that must be closely monitored. These SKUs have different roles; for instance, a ₹5 SKU (28g of Parle-G pack) may be the one customers first choose when they would like to try the biscuit for the first time and a ₹10

(100g of Parle-G pack) may become the SKU most often purchased by regular customers. Here, a marketer decides the role of each SKU and assesses if more such SKUs are needed to be introduced in the market to grow the business.

Diagnosing Brand Challenges

To do a good job of managing a brand, a brand manager or marketer is expected to observe a set of variables. Ideally, a marketer should look at an infinite number of variables. For example, a marketer looks at macro-economic factors that may not have immediate impact on the product such as GDP growth, employment, global commodity rates, as well as inflation. However, some key variables listed below are the ones a marketer must look at in order of priority:

1. **Consumer Measures:** This involves a set of reports that are made available on monthly or quarterly basis to inform a brand executive on the health of the brand from a consumer's perspective. These measures are usually bucketed under three heads:

    • **Salience:** These typically include measures of awareness which are often linked to mental and physical availability of the consumer. Mental availability is ensured through Above the Line (ATL) communication (this includes advertising), while physical availability is ensured through distribution and visibility in stores. Brands like Colgate, Cadbury, Lux Soap, etc., are salient in our mind because we regularly see their advertisements on TV as well as in the stores we visit.

- **Consideration:** Consideration is a measure of 'intention to purchase', and could be linked to product or proposition performance; essentially how desirable is the product for a shopper or consumer to buy or purchase it.
- **Behaviour:** Behaviour measures are closest to market reality and inform us if all the actions undertaken in pushing the brand will eventually result in the consumer claiming to have purchased the product or not.

Understanding consumer health scores also helps a marketer decode how the current mix is performing and if at all there is a need to make any modifications in brand's strategy to drive a better performance. The current mix here refers to the current product formulation, its pricing against the competition, regular presence in advertising as well as its presence in stores. It's important to note that the consumer health data is collected at a 'claimed level', as in, a sample of consumers who claimed to have been impacted by the brand.

2. **Market Share Data:** The market share data is more real and presents a sharper reflection of the actual competitive position of the brand in the market. Some of the key parameters that a marketer looks at to understand the brand's competitive position includes:

- **Market share:** The share of the market captured by the brand. This can be looked at either in volume or value.
- **Numeric distribution or weighted distribution:** This tells us how easily the product is available versus the

availability of the overall category. Often, weighted distribution is a better metric as it informs us if we are in the 'right' outlets, or the outlets where the bulk of the category is getting sold in.

- **Per Dealer Offtakes (PDO):** A market share growth or decline can either be because of the shift in the availability or change in the amount of stock sold in a store. And, hence, per dealer offtakes or PDO is a measure of the stock sold per store.
- **Share among handlers:** This is a measure of the market share that a brand has only within the universe of stores that the product is available in.
- **Stock Turnaround Ratio (STR):** This metric indicates approximately the number of days the stock is being held across the market.

All these metrics help a marketer understand how well the brand is selling and the challenges to address in order to improve its business position.

3. **Internal Sales Numbers:** This data is readily available to any marketer and helps them study the volume or value growth by pack type across channels and geographies. Here, the marketer studies the distribution performance and the impact of promotions run.

4. **Profit and Loss Statement:** This is eventually the most important 'report card' for any marketer where they can study not just the top line (gross sales) but also the bottom line (net profit) delivered by the business they manage. There are a number of variables here, including the packaging material cost, raw material cost of the recipe,

sales and distribution expenses, and advertising and sales-promotion spends that they can study to understand how to improve brand's performance.

Above and beyond these metrics, the marketer is also expected to be on top of a host of competitive intelligence practices which include the nutritional panel, recipe details, new launches, pricing position versus completion, and so on. For beginners, however, mentioned above are the key data pieces that a marketer must look at on a monthly basis.

Performance Measures

Speaking of performance metric, a salesperson would be well aware of the business and market share targets, but a marketer needs to familiarize oneself with a different metric, that is, operating income (OI) or the profitability of the brand.

> A marketer takes on the responsibility of the profit and loss statement of a brand. Hence, the right definition of a brand manager would be that of an entrepreneur running the business model of the brand.

An example of the interrelationship of various mix elements such as product quality, pricing, advertising spends, and distribution reach can be seen by comparing and contrasting the strategies of Amul Kool Flavoured Milk, Britannia's Winkin' Cow, and Hershey's Milkshakes. While Amul Kool offers thinner milk drink at just ₹20 and Winkin' Cow offers a thicker milkshake at ₹30, Hershey's tries to own an even more premium position at ₹35. However, here, Hershey's supports the mix with aggressive advertising and in-store investments.

Thus, a brand manager must keep an eye on three crucial metrics: (i) sales targets taken at the start of the year, (ii) competition activations to ensure their brand grows in market share, and most importantly, (iii) ensuring that both of the targets are delivered without compromising on profits.

A brand manager, therefore, has a number of levers at their disposal, including the recipe cost, pricing, activation spends, and so on, with the eventual purpose of delivering an effective business model.

Creating or Developing a Brand Vision

> While most of the factors covered above are specific to the performance of a brand, a true marketer is the one who is also able to set a vision for where they want their brand to reach.

This is the hardest and the most important task of a brand custodian, and often, is considered more of an art than science.

This takes me back to the time when I was appointed as the brand manager for Cadbury Gems, one of the smallest brands of Mondelez India. After assuming the position, I realized that the brand communication for this product came across as kiddie—suitable for kids. I reached out to my line manager and shared that Gems has a far bigger potential than we give it credit for. For instance, M&M's, the chocolate candies originated in the United States and are similar to

Gems, makes four times better business than all of Cadbury Chocolates globally put together. This inspired me to build a larger vision or ambition I had for Gems.

On a similar note, a close friend of mine, who was the brand manager for Cadbury 5 Star in 2008, then believed that the chocolate bar has the potential to become a 'youth icon' (this was way before the brand came up with their popular and funny Ramesh-Suresh advertisement series). While it seemed audacious that a chocolate brand could ever compete with the likes of Coke or Pepsi, arguably so, 5 Star indeed delivered to that vision.

Therefore, much like a founder of a start-up who begins with a larger-than-life vision for their business, a brand manager must think long and hard about the potential their brand holds, first from one's own perspective, then from the perspective of the organization and finally from consumer's perspective. This, I believe, is the most important task of a brand custodian.

The Marketer's Checklist

- A brand manager or marketer should be able to focus on the health of the business determined by profitability.
- A marketer should be able to manage the entire mix, including product, price, place, and promotions.
- A marketer should be able to manage the brand holistically by studying consumer-facing measures, market performance, as well as business metrics like profitability.
- Remember, the key contribution from the marketer or the brand custodian is to set a compelling vision for the brand.

BUILDING A CATEGORY STRATEGY

As brand custodians of Cadbury Celebrations, we had introduced 26 different packs. I often wondered then whether the consumer even cared about different colours, shapes, and sizes that we sell our packs in. Finding an answer to this question helped me unlock the business growth that doubled the brand sales between 2008 and 2012. A few years later, when I joined Britannia in 2017, I was surprised to see that a promotional pricing strategy of providing 20% extra in products could shift sales more than advertising ever would. I figured that the consumer shopping behaviour varies across product categories quite meaningfully.

As I worked across diverse product categories—chocolates, biscuits, dairy, and alcohol—I understood that the business model for each of these categories is quite different. While chocolates and premium alcohol are sold at high prices, they also require a lot of brand investments in the form of advertising or in-store marketing to drive offtakes. On the other hand, biscuits and dairy products often operate at lower prices and are driven through the right pricing for the winning product.

Role of Categories

> In order to understand how and why the
> business model for each of the product
> categories are different, we must understand
> the profit and loss statement of the organization
> and how their product categories operate.

We must understand this simple fundamental principle of marketing: all products are eventually the sum of their functional and emotional benefits.

Product categories, which we also refer to as essentials or commodities, see almost all of their value being attributed to their functional benefits. Functional benefits of a product can be accounted by the Cost of Goods Sold (COGS) or the physical aspects of the ingredients and the cost of making the same. Since these benefits are easily replicable, the cost of a branded product in comparison to the loose version of the same product may not vary widely. Hence, little money would be required to be spent in brand building.

However, personal care products further fall into the 'want' and 'need' categories. These categories—centered around the emotional benefits a consumer derives from a product—help a consumer look and feel good. A good approximate of a product's emotional benefits are derived from long-term investments in advertising and brand building. This is the reason why personal care products are heavily advertised as compared to other products like atta (flour), dal (lentils), and salt. There is a huge emotional angle to their purchases and this, therefore, results in heavy monetary investment in the brand building of these products.

To further explain this concept, day-to-day necessities such as bread, eggs, salt, pulses don't see much brand building as limited differentiation is expected between competing brands. These products tend to belong to the 'need' category. However, categories like chocolates, alcohol, and fragrances see a lot of brand building investments like advertising as these fall under 'want' categories. A marketer needs to seed a thought within you that you desire these products. This desire to buy a 'want' category may be created from a functional lens, say in case of Cadbury Silk, the droolworthy images inspire a need to indulge yourself. Similarly, marketers can 'create' wants through an emotional lens. For instance, Johnnie Walker whisky brand may create a want to celebrate moments of success by sipping a branded liquor that is an epitome of pride. Similarly, wearing a popular perfume brand may create a sense of confidence when you are heading on a date, and so on.

From the perspective of a profit and loss statement of a brand, in most cases, product categories in the market (centered around functional benefits) eventually deliver the same bottom line (operating or net profit) of 10-15%. Whereas, the cost of goods sold and essentials might contribute to as much as 50-70% of the top line (net sales value (NSV)) and the expenditure on advertising and brand building might be as low as 1-5%. However, in the case of non-discretionary product categories like personal care, the cost of goods sold (COGS) might be as low as 15-30% while the expenditure on advertising can be set as high as 15-50% leading to similar levels of net profits.

This helps us understand that products categories (focusing mainly on emotional benefits) like personal care need heavy advertising and brand building followed by impulse categories (products which are bought on impulse) like chocolates and aerated beverages, salty snacks, and biscuits, and so on. Essentials like *atta* (flour), pulses, lentils, salt, etc., need the least brand building and, hence, have the least ability to command a premium over and above the cost of production.

The Purchase Decision Hierarchy

Now that we know the difference between various categories, as a marketer, we also need to perceive how important each part of the mix is to the consumer. Therefore, we need to understand an interesting consumer study—often commissioned by the consumer insights team—called as the 'Purchase Decision Hierarchy' or PDH.

> The PDH helps reveal the order and importance of each part of the mix which often includes brand, flavour, sub-category (variants), price, promotion, pack shape, design, product category, functional claims, and so on.

A PDH study further helps a marketer understand the order in which a customer evaluates benefits. For example, in the case of automobiles, the first decision that a customer might make is the budget followed by the category of cars and then perhaps the brand. However, in the case of chocolates, a customer may choose from the category of a chocolate bar like Cadbury Dairy Milk or a wafer bar like Kit Kat or Perk may come first, and so on.

As it can be expected, in categories like personal care, 'the brand' might be the most important factor. However, in categories like salt, a product benefit (for instance, iodized versus non-iodized salt) might tip the balance in terms of consumer preference.

I would like to share an interesting example of how such a PDH study has helped me decode the mix during my time at Cadbury Celebrations as its brand manager. Since we believed that shoppers value novelty the most when it comes to gifting, we would introduce new packs every year and aggressively invest in their various shapes and sizes. When I took over the portfolio, we already had 26 different Cadbury Celebrations packs that we manufactured throughout the year. However, the PDH study that we commissioned revealed that the consumer is actually driven to purchase by three key factors—sub-category, brand, and price. So, either the consumer would choose between *mithai* (sweets), dry fruits, chocolate gift pack, biscuits gift pack, or be swayed by the brand name (a Cadbury vs. Ferrero Rocher choice), or decide their purchase based on the price bands. Attributes like design, shape or size of the pack, or the type of chocolates included in the pack made no difference to their preferences. Hence, over the next four years of my duration as the brand manager, I reduced the number of SKUs from 26 to merely 6 thereby reducing the inventory cost of different packs and consequently doubling the Cadbury gifting business.

However, not all food categories get this similar treatment by the consumers. In the case of an adjacent category of biscuits, we might find that a consumer may be propelled to shift brands within the same category by a different flavour or promotion. Hence in biscuits, you may observe that the pack colours are led by the flavour and not the brand.

Take for instance Britannia Good Day Cashew Cookies or Sunfeast Mom's Magic Cashew & Almond Cookies; they are both orange in colour. Here, the consumer possibly sees almond as the deciding factor in choosing either of the two brands. This hypothesis might also be the reason why Maska Chaska is a preferred variant of Britannia 50-50 and might often hold more equity than the brand '50-50' itself. Furthermore, since biscuits are often stocked at home, a customer may give higher preference to a price discount so that they may purchase a larger quantity and stock the same at home. On the other hand, if we take the case of chocolates, since they are bought to satisfy a momentary craving, price discounts may not drive preference with customers.

This establishes that a thorough understanding of purchase decision hierarchy is critical for brand managers in building their marketing mixes even before other variables like innovation or advertising needs kick in.

Role of Stock Keeping Units (SKUs)

A marketer creates a portfolio of offers or 'stock keeping units' (different pack sizes) that cater to different occasions or consumer needs. As you would have noticed, most brands have several SKUs (stock keeping units) at different grammages and price points. For instance, the most commonly sold bar of Lux soap (100g) may be priced at ₹36, while there might also be a pack of a larger soap bar (150g) priced at ₹66. You may also come across a family pack or combo pack of four bars with a 'Buy 4+1 free' offer. This invites an obvious question: why do we see so many types of packs and what is their key purpose?

Lead Pack: The lead pack—one that offers standard brand insight—is normally considered as a 'hero SKU' and is most often utilized for promotional purposes. Among chocolates, best example for a lead pack would be the 40 g bar of Cadbury Dairy Milk as it offers the best utilization experience. While in biscuits, most of the times, a ₹10 pack (for e.g., 50 g of Britannia Marie Gold), and in health drinks, 500 g of Bournvita jar or a pouch work best as a lead pack for their respective categories.

Penetration Packs: While the lead pack offers the best quality brand experience, it may not be the bestselling SKU. In a nation like India where affordability is most of the time the biggest obstruction to the adoption of new categories like shampoos or chocolates, a reasonable pack, often, becomes the highest-selling SKU; an apt example for this is shampoo sachets costing 50 paisa and ₹1. However, most companies could struggle to make reasonable profits on such SKUs and, hence, they may need a more affordable recipe cost.

Up-trade Pack: The most affordable SKU may be the one that is adopted at first but may not provide the most satisfying experience to the user. Hence, an up-trade pack at a higher grammage is usually introduced. For example, a ₹5 bar of Cadbury Dairy Milk may provide just a quick taste of the chocolate, but a ₹10 bar may be far more satiating. A higher-priced SKU allows the manufacturer to garner more value for their efforts and grow their business and profit margins.

Family Pack: Marketers are aware that usually customers require three-four soaps to last an entire month, and to satiate this requirement, they may purchase different bars from different companies frequently during the month. So, to block out other competitive brands from entering the customers' cupboards, marketers offer them a family pack at a discount, say, Buy 3+1 Free offer or 20% free. Although this family pack is sold at a discount, it enables the marketer to garner all the sales of such households for a month and beat their competition.

Super Saver or Modern Trade Packs: In recent times, marketers have realized that customers may visit large format stores like DMart and Spencer's Retail looking for deals and may buy goods that may last them for couple of months. In such cases, companies launch extra-large packs and sell them at a heavy discount. For instance, for one kg pack of biscuits a customer would get a major discount of 50%. These are usually termed as Super Saver Packs or Modern Trade Pack.

Understanding the role of your SKUs is, therefore, vital to building your classification methodology.

Category Strategy

Let's now understand how a marketer or a business head goes about making a category strategy for the overall business which includes a portfolio of brands and not just one brand. The marketer's job is to deliver business results by creating a marketing mix (product, price, place, and promotions) which ensures their brands enter customer households and are also consumed substantially. The steps to achieve the same can be termed as category strategy as it paves the way for a category of products to grow within a given market. The key tasks that help achieve the same are:

Market Penetration

This is often one of the most important and difficult tasks for any product category as it means driving behavioural change in non-users to try a new offering. This is often exclusively a market leader's task as introducing a category into new households is expensive and requires resources from across the organization, including product development, sales and distribution, marketing, and supply infrastructure. A few examples of how this task can be accomplished are:

1. Creation of new SKUs at a penetrative price. For instance, launch of shampoo sachets by certain brands allowed shampoo as a category to enter the households which had never bought a shampoo earlier as they couldn't afford a full bottle of the same shampoo.
2. Building cultural relevance: This is something that Cadbury has done effectively by positioning itself as the

modern-day *mithai* brand resulting in households (which might have only ever bought a pack of regular *mithai* during Diwali) gifting boxes of Cadbury Celebrations instead.

3. Distribution expansions through newer distribution models: This is in order to reach new customers; something that a company like Unilever is known for pioneering thereby reaching the smallest towns in the country. It is this approach that has allowed products like soaps, shampoo sachets, tea, and salt pouches to reach households deep within the rural markets of our country.

Frequency

Once a consumer has tried an offering (a specific SKU), the next step for a marketer is to enable the consumer to consume the same offering multiple times. This can be done by introducing new SKUs with different packaging formats or flavour variants that cater to new reasons for consuming the same product. A few examples that demonstrate the same are:

1. Cadbury Dairy Milk Home Pack was also positioned to the customers as *meetha* (a post-dinner dessert) through advertisements. Presenting Dairy Milk as a dessert created another occasion in addition to the consumption of Dairy Milk chocolates during the day.

2. Festival-specific packs like the *thandai* launched by Paper Boat makes that product variant extremely relevant during Holi. Similarly, 'plum cakes' are more relevant during Christmas. Festivals, therefore, offer an opportunity of adding new occasions to a product category.

3. Introducing Pepsi 'Swag' can, which is narrower in its design, is yet another example of an addition of a new occasion to the product. It was advertised in the market keeping in mind teenagers who would feel cool about themselves by drinking Pepsi in these 'swag' cans in their college cafeteria.

Average Weight of Purchase

In this category task, a brand might encourage a consumer to purchase or consume more in an existing occasion. This is a relatively simple behavioural change which is often brought in by introducing family packs or super saver packs. This is where the role of SKUs we discussed in the previous section becomes relevant.

Average Value of Purchase

This, again, is a relatively difficult task, but one that holds a lot of promise for brand building and evolution of consumer habits. This task is essentially about convincing an existing brand consumer to consider a more expensive product or a higher quality experience in the same consumption occasion. The up-trade task that Colgate does well of moving consumers from their existing Colgate Strong Teeth Toothpaste to their more expensive toothpastes with different functionalities is a best example of this task. Consumers could move from Colgate Strong Teeth to Colgate Active Salt or Colgate Sensitive Teeth or Colgate Total seeking benefits that they are willing to spend more money on.

Cross-Selling

The fifth and the final category task that a marketer needs to build the business plan for is to cross-sell, i.e., sell adjacent categories such as toothbrushes and mouthwashes along with the core category of toothpastes into the same consumer household. This task is very important as it helps a brand extend its business beyond its own category and increase the business that can be captured from a given household.

In a nutshell, before making a detailed marketing strategy, one must first understand the category of a product and build a business strategy. This helps us understand how categories differ from one another, the role of purchase decision hierarchy in understanding various brand levers, role of SKUs, and how to develop category strategy.

The Marketer's Checklist

In order to create a category strategy, the following steps need to be followed:

- We must first understand the nature of the category we are dealing with. While commodities are low-margin category driven by needs of items like *atta* (flour), salt, etc., impulse categories are 'want' categories with good margins but also require higher investments.
- Next, we must try and understand the hierarchy of decisions that a shopper or consumer makes while purchasing a particular product. This could include variables like price, brand, design, ingredients, and so on.
- All brands exist through a number of packs or SKUs. It's

important for us to understand the role of each pack to ensure we do the right pricing thereby driving optimal business gains.

- Finally, a category strategy leads to the tasks which the brand must perform in order to grow, including driving penetration, frequency, average weight of purchase, average value of purchase, or cross-selling.

HOW IS A BRAND STRATEGY BUILT?

While a category strategy helps us understand the lay of the land, the task that most of us are entrusted with as marketers is to build a strategy for our individual brands. While I was leading brands such as Cadbury Dairy Milk and Cadbury Celebrations—already established segment leaders—the key task here for me was often to drive category expansion. However, while managing Britannia's Dairy category, stealing the share from existing competition was more of a priority for me.

We will dive deeper into specifics of the strategy in terms of making advertising or launching innovations in subsequent sections. Here, we will focus primarily on the overall strategy and key steps that a brand person must navigate to build a strong brand strategy.

In my experience, there are just four key steps to plan your brand's marketing strategy:

1. Uncovering your brand's task
2. Understanding your consumer
3. Figuring out what to say
4. Creating the marketing plan

1. Uncovering your brand's task

The brand task is the basis for all strategy and this task is often a resultant of the organizational strategy. Now, of course, all of us want to achieve business growth and gain market share. However, in my experience, the two key brand tasks are:

You either grow the category

or

You steal market share!

Growing the category is usually the task chosen by market leaders like Coca Cola or Cadbury Dairy Milk. It is relevant when you already have a large share of the category and if the category grows, you get most of the benefit! It's this task that leads to magical campaigns like *'Kuch Meetha Ho Jaye'* or *'Thanda Matlab Coca Cola'*. Here, you basically source business from outside your category. Thus, chocolates become a modern-day *'mithai'* or Coca Cola takes on the roadside juice, butter milk, or *lassi*.

Stealing market share is often a strategy that is practised by the followers, but it's no less exciting. However, here you are clear that you are sourcing business from within the category. For instance, when Fogg perfume positioned itself as a 'no gas, only liquid' deodorant with '800 guaranteed sprays', it stole the thunder from every other deodorant brand. Similarly, One Plus took away the premium mobile market from Apple providing groundbreaking product innovation at competitive prices.

There is a reason why these two tasks are the most crucial for building a strong brand strategy. Consumers don't really care about brands, what they care about is product categories; the brand that understands them then becomes a surrogate for those categories. Like when we say 'Xerox' we essentially mean to 'photocopy'. Similarly, a Lux Soap becomes the surrogate for the category of soaps for consumers who seek glamour in their personal care offerings, while brands like Rexona or Santoor may need to convince the consumers why they must reevaluate their choices through their 'steal market share' task.

2. Understanding your consumer

> Once you are done with figuring out 'what'
> you want to do, you have to next figure out
> 'who' you want to target.

Therefore, the next few important steps to consider are segmentation, targeting, and positioning.

So, now you try and cut the market into different consumer groups that you wish to target. You can do this through marketing demographics or observing consumer attitude. Take for instance the case of Tata Nano Car; an ideal target group would comprise the ones who currently ride scooters and can be convinced that they can now improve their lifestyle and afford a small car. Or, you could even target people who already own cars and convince them to buy another one for their spouses or children.

However, the key task here is to identify the parameters that drive these differences in usage. Who is that 'bullseye consumer' you wish to target? So, are you targeting kids, teens, or adults? Are you targeting the affluent consumers or the masses? Those living in small towns or mega metros?

Once, you identify the target consumer segment, you should think about how to position your offering. This is done by studying the positioning of your competition that is most differentiated and most compelling to your target group. If we look at the juice market, Dabur's Real Juices primarily targets kids and tells mothers to give their kids Real Juice instead of cold drinks, on the other hand, Tropicana targets the youth and tells them that Tropicana is an ideal accompaniment to a healthy lifestyle.

3. Figuring out what to say

Once you are certain about your positioning, you then rope in the bright talent from the advertising creative team who can help you figure out the most engaging way to communicate the brand's positioning to the consumers. In the case of Cadbury Silk, you know that you wish to position your brand as a distinctly indulgent offering, the creative team, therefore, arrives at an idea of dramatizing how beautifully the chocolate melts.

4. Creating a marketing plan

You now have your budgets allocated and are perfectly clear on the one thing you want to say that will drive your brand's business; so, how do you deploy that money? There are broadly four buckets where you can invest—advertising, consumer engagement, shopper marketing, and innovation.

Advertising is, of course, the term most of us are familiar with. It is basically communicating your core proposition to consumers. Simply put, convincing your consumers with the one thing that will make all the difference. Like an Axe Deo Ad saying: You don't need to bother with body odour as the girls will see you as an eye candy! Or, a Cadbury Silk Ad saying: It is the tastiest, meltiest chocolate ever!

However, today, consumer engagement is growing exponentially. It is basically about figuring out your consumer's passion and participating within it in a manner that can be owned by your brand. For e.g., hundreds of brands participated in 'Vocal for Local' initiative by Govt. of India, but only Tata Salt seemed credible, as it has been positioning itself as '*Desh ka namak*' for the longest time.

Also, shopper marketing has a large role to play in marketing strategy, where you basically make the retail space an extension of the world of the brand; Apple does it in their fabulous stores or the way several brands follow this strategy in supermarkets.

Lastly, optimizing innovation and introducing new products are an ideal way to express your brand proposition, as long as you extend the core of your brand and not try to become the competition. Cadbury Dairy Milk, for instance, expanding its core to Cadbury Silk is a great idea, but when brands try and steal from their competition by copying them, it rarely leads to great results.

Building a robust marketing strategy can take anywhere between a few months to a year. It starts with having clarity on what you are setting out to achieve, followed by an understanding of who your consumer is, the distinct benefit you wish to offer to the consumer, and how you wish to communicate that difference. The entire process is rich and rewarding and carried out in collaborating with your agency partners. However, the end result can be some brilliant innovation, clutter-breaking communication, or an exciting brand activation. The strategy is successful only if it leads to tangible business results and helps you deliver your brand tasks.

Now that you have a bird's eye view into the entire process, the subsequent sections of the book will delve deeper into each of these spaces and help you appreciate all of the tasks required to achieve them.

The Marketer's Checklist

- The four key steps to create your brand's marketing strategy are:
  1. Uncovering your brand's task
  2. Understanding your consumer
  3. Figuring out what to say
  4. Creating a marketing plan
- The two key brand tasks are:
  1. Grow the category
  2. Steal market share
- Understanding the consumer includes 'segmentation', 'targeting', and 'positioning'.
- Figuring out what to say is about landing the right 'positioning' for your brand.
- Creating strong marketing plans includes judicious investments into advertising, consumer engagement, shopper marketing, and innovation.

CRAFTING A BRAND PURPOSE

Once a brand strategy has been built, the most magical part of a brand's core is the brand purpose. Arriving at a brand purpose requires deeper understanding of the product and services and also the consumers.

Personally speaking, the concept of brand purpose was most powerfully brought to life during my stint at Diageo India—a brand which had then defined its organizational purpose as 'Celebrating life, every day, everywhere'. This essentially means that Diageo India is the consumers' partner in socializing and celebrations.

At its core, brand purpose means uncovering the reason for the existence of your product or service and the larger reason for your brand to exist. Not only is this concept crucial for a seamless business strategy but it also ensures a consistent set of values that builds loyalty with your consumers.

In this section, we shall understand the genesis of the term and how it links to your business and consumer strategy.

Start with 'Why'

One of the most watched TED talks in the world is the one given by English-American author and motivational speaker

Simon Sinek in 2009. As on March 2024, the talk—Start with 'Why'—garnered over 11 million views. The talk essentially encapsulates a simple fact that consumers are moved by 'why' your brand exists rather than 'what it does'.

The brilliant example that Simon Sinek gives is that of Apple. Being one of the largest tech companies, Apple doesn't tell you to buy its products simply because they are made with cutting-edge technology and great design. They rather tell you that "We believe in challenging the status quo and the way we challenge the status quo is by making products that are not just beautifully-designed, but are also simple to use and user-friendly."

This concept is of great personal relevance to me, because when I tried to craft my 'personal purpose', I realized that I thrive in making connections and solving problems by connecting people. At Diageo India, I crafted my personal purpose as 'I exist to create magic through collaboration with others'. This has been my personal credo at Diageo India and all the other companies I worked with.

At Cadbury, the magic that was created for Cadbury Celebrations was through the proposition of *'Toh Iss Diwali Aap Kise Khush Karenge?'* where we changed our focus from what the box consists to the reason why it exists, that is, to enable the gifter to delight the receiver.

The consumers are, therefore, moved by 'why' your brand exists and not just by 'what' its features are. While this is a compelling concept, interestingly enough, it is already linked to a concept called the 'Brand Ladder' that most students are taught in their management institutes or B-schools.

The Brand Ladder

The brand ladder interestingly starts from the
'what' or what your product's features are,
and then makes it way up to the 'benefits'
it delivers. As we move further upwards the
ladder, it leads to the consumer rewards or
'how it makes the consumer feel?'. Then,
further up it leads to the emotional benefits or
'shared values and beliefs', or essentially
'why' it exists.

Let me demonstrate this through the example of one of the world's strongest brands—Coca Cola.

Features: Coke is essentially a dark carbonated, sugary beverage.

Benefits: Consuming Coke is refreshing and leads to a sugar rush.

Consumer rewards: The sugar and the carbonation refreshes you and makes you feel happy.

However, the real magic that Coke has woven for over a century is that they have managed to transcend the boundaries of just a product and have chosen to talk about 'Open Happiness' alluding to a harmonious world.

It is the shared values of harmony, optimism, and joy that endears Coca Cola as a brand to so many consumers across the world. The joy one feels triggers the emotional centres of the brain and makes Coke such a valuable brand.

Understanding Your Product's Features and Benefits

Given that uncovering your brand purpose is fundamentally about finding the right positioning, a marketer needs to start by interrogating how your product is different from your competition. Often the differentiation might even be quite slight. However, by adding appropriate RTBs (Reasons to Believe), a marketer can carve out a distinct position.

Let's study a few popular brands and discuss how they are able to differentiate their products from their competition by adding interesting features or RTBs.

The most common example is that of Coca Cola, Pepsi, and Thums Up. All the three beverages have much in common and only the most discerning consumer may be able to call out the difference in a blind taste challenge. Now, while Coke positions itself as 'the Real Thing', Pepsi needs to find a positioning which is rooted in a product difference. The fact is Pepsi is slightly sweeter than Coke and they then took that point of difference to position themselves as the 'choice of the new generation'. Thums Up, on the other hand, has higher carbonation and is less sweet and that enabled them to take the position of an intensely masculine drink with brand ambassadors like Salman Khan, the Indian film actor known for portraying macho characters on screen.

Now, if we look at Lux, Santoor, and Dettol, I can say from my previous work experience that 99% of the soaps are made from exactly the same ingredients. However, Lux soap brand uses glamorous fragrances and heavy advertising to position themselves as the choice of Bollywood superstars thereby collaborating with actors ranging from Katrina Kaif, Alia Bhatt, Deepika Padukone, Kareena Kapoor as their brand ambassadors in the recent past. Santoor uses beneficial properties of sandal and turmeric as a way to build a story of woman with younger-looking skin. The brand has come up with numerous editions of ads that show a married woman who doesn't look her age, but is married and with a child. On the other hand, Dettol uses its parent brand of antiseptics to talk about protection from germs.

In the toothpaste category, for instance, Dabur Red toothpaste calls itself as the best Ayurvedic toothpaste for various dental problems, while Colgate has always emphasized that it is the brand recommended by dentists. Closeup is positioned on the Fresh Breath platform owing to its gel-based formulation.

It's, therefore, evident that the first step in the journey of finding your brand's purpose is to understand the brand's features and ladder it up to a clear functional benefit. Here, when I use the word 'ladder up', I essentially mean making a logical connection from attributes to functional benefits to emotional benefits. To elaborate, most consumers are aware that 'salt' was traditionally used to clean ones teeth, so a toothpaste that has salt as an attribute may have the functional benefit of cleaning your teeth better and also provide the emotional benefits of confidence in your dental hygiene.

Understanding Your Consumer

Once a marketer clearly understands what sets their product apart from the competition, they can uncover what drives consumers' preference by deconstructing the attitude, mood, and beliefs of their consumers that causes them to buy the product. A few interesting case studies of brands that have found a compelling purpose and how it links to those products is what we shall discuss next.

One of the earliest marketing campaigns that comes to my mind the moment 'purpose' is mentioned, is that of Dove's by Unilever. Dove has been running a fantastic campaign of 'Real Beauty' since 2004. However, one might wonder what gives Dove the right to talk about 'real beauty'? The fact that a bar of Dove soap basically contains mild cleansers and moisturising cream that cleanses the skin rather than any fragrances or harsh compounds that might harm the skin is where the brand's credibility comes from.

In 2022, during one of the recent editions of the same campaign, Dove asked its consumers to #StopTheBeautyTest through a film in collaboration with a well-known Ad agency Ogilvy. The film showcases how young girls in India are forced and groomed according to the standards of its patriarchal society. Through this campaign, Dove sent out a crucial message to the country that they should stop subjecting their women to a 'beauty test' that makes them feel unbeautiful and crushes their self-esteem.

During COVID-19 pandemic, in 2021, Lifebuoy launched a series of public health messages such as 'It's In Your Hands' by roping in experts who appealed to the people that they should regularly wash their hands with *any* soap (not just Lifebuoy) and maintain hygiene precautions (physical distancing, wearing masks). Consumers, therefore, saw Lifebuoy as the brand that champions washing one's hands regularly throughout the pandemic. This comes naturally because the soap brand has espoused the cause of health and hygiene for several years now, thereby making Lifebuoy the natural first choice for any such needs.

To give you another example, one of the most powerful purpose-driven campaigns in the past few years has been that of P&G's laundry brand Ariel. The #ShareTheLoad campaign talks about the existing inequality within the Indian households. It lays emphasis on the stress a homemaker (in most cases, a woman) goes through due to the gendered expectations to perform domestic chores and urges their spouses to contribute more, to 'share the load' equally. The fact that P&G has an array of products that has made life easier for homemakers for years now gives them the credibility to talk about these issues.

In fact, in 2022, Ariel launched its fifth edition of #ShareTheLoad campaign exploring different gendered themes. In 2015, when the campaign was first launched, it asked the question: 'Is laundry only a woman's job?'. In 2016, the campaign asked fathers to pledge in contributing to the household chores by saying—Dads #ShareTheLoad. In the year 2019, they focussed on the upbringing of sons, asking the core question: do we raise our sons the same way, with the same values we raise our daughters? In 2020, it was about #SharingTheLoad for equal sleep underlining the message that how the unequal distribution of household chores negatively impacts the sleep of Indian women (in most cases) more than their husbands. The ad further stressed that it's important for the men to step up and share the load equally so that their wives are not deprived of sleep. The latest 2022 ad film #ShareTheLoad to #SeeEqual talks about seeing the spouse equally because when 'you see equal, you share equal'. It highlights the deeply-embedded unconscious bias men tend to have while carrying out housework.

It is, therefore, crucial to deeply understand the attitude and beliefs of your consumers. This in-depth understanding, which has the potential to drive behavioural changes in your consumers, is called Insight—the crucial key to uncover your brand's purpose. Once you are able to champion a cause that your consumers can deeply connect with, through an empathetic and meaningful insight, you start your journey of uncovering your purpose.

Finding Your Purpose

> While a 'purpose' deeply moves your consumers and can build loyalty through a connection, it also turns into a responsibility as you then offer a yardstick for consumers to measure your authenticity. Once a brand articulates a purpose or a clear 'point of view', consumers expect consistency.

Some of the brands that have managed to achieve this feat:

1. **Tata Tea:** One of the most famous purpose-driven campaigns in India include '*Jaago Re*' from Tata Tea. This ad leveraged the simple benefit of drinking tea as a beverage by showing how the caffeine in it wakes you up to the purpose thereby awakening your morality. They have been remarkably consistent over years and have done a fabulous job.

2. **Britannia Marie:** Known as one of India's oldest brands, Britannia's Marie Lite Biscuits variant for long has been the favourite choice of women for their 10 a.m. tea time. Thousands of Indian housewives long for this 'me-time hour' every morning once their husbands leave for work and the kids go to school. It's also the time when a housewife wonders if she can do something more for herself other than take care of the domestic chores and perform parental duties. The marketers at Britannia tapped into this aspect of individuality and launched the Marie 'My Start-up' contest to provide seed funding to aspiring women entrepreneurs thereby encouraging them to think about themselves.

    This has perhaps been Britannia's most successful activation which has delivered solid growth to the brand and improved its affinity with women. So much so that the brand has invested in this contest for three editions with a total of 3.8 million entries till date and targeted another 2 million entries in 2023 for its fourth edition.

This establishes that once brands deeply understand their consumers, they can craft a compelling purpose that builds brand's loyalty and preference.

Rules of a Good Purpose

Now, there can potentially be hundreds, if not thousands, of purposes that brands can try and own. How do you know that you have found something that your consumers will value and benefit your brand as well? Here is a simple checklist:

1. Your brand must have the credibility of owning the

purpose. There must be something specific about your product's legacy that offers credibility. It's the philanthropic nature of the Tata Group that allows them to pull off campaigns like '*Jaago Re*' that inspire social change. However, when Gillette tried to talk about toxic masculinity channelling #MeToo movement through their 'We believe: the best men can be' razors commercials, they faced severe backlash from consumers who questioned what exactly gives them the right to talk about such a sensitive subject.

2. The purpose your brand has decided to own must have a link to why your consumers prefer your product. For example, no one will be surprised to hear Patanjali Ayurved talk about natural goodness or Ayurveda given the nature of their portfolio and the values that yoga guru Baba Ramdev espouses. However, at the same time, Colgate would never appear credible if they talk about natural formulations.

3. Ideally, the purpose should be something that consumers can't do on their own and would like to feel that they are a part of a larger movement by supporting a brand. Tanishq, for instance, has often talked about breaking the stereotypes their consumers might themselves not entirely feel empowered to do so. For example, in their 2013 ad film, Tanishq talked about celebrating second marriages. Here, the ad film tries to portray that people, especially a woman with a child, marrying for the second time is often judged by society and is hesitant towards celebrating her second marriage socially. The ad film posits a society where such marriages can be celebrated and socially-accepted with an open mind. Therefore,

in making their brand choice, the consumers feel empowered that they are a part of a larger positive social change—something that the brand wishes to harness their energy towards.

To sum up, the purpose of a brand is a powerful concept of brand building as loyalty and preference is finally based on how a brand makes the consumer feel rather than providing mere tangible benefits of its product's quality or performance. However, a marketer must first deeply understand the brand's differentiators and then link the same to the values and beliefs of its core target group. Post this, as a brand adopts a consistent tone of voice and delivers actions that its target group believes in, it successfully manages to build its credibility and loyalty.

The Marketer's Checklist

The brand's purpose lies at the core of its reason for existence and clarity on the same impacts all brand-related decisions a brand custodian drives. The steps to be followed in uncovering the brand's purpose includes:

- Thorough understanding of the product's attributes, features, and benefits.
- An in-depth knowledge of the consumer's beliefs, attitudes, and behaviour.
- Finding the brand's purpose by drawing a clear link between the product's functional differentiators and the emotions benefits which the consumers are seeking.
- Building a credible purpose supported by brand communications and brand actions which lend credibility to the brand's point of view.

2

UNDERSTANDING THE CONSUMER

Consumer Behaviour

Segmentation

Creating Consumer Portrait

Uncovering Consumer Insight

Brand Concept

CONSUMER BEHAVIOUR

One of the biggest lessons I learnt when I entered brand management was how little consumers cared about brands. Of course, for a marketer, their brand is the center of their world; we literally live and breathe our brands. However, it's always a bit of a shock when we meet consumers and realize that they are barely aware of our brands. Even the most loyal users may be purchasing a brand over decades by force of habit and nothing more. Upon quizzing the consumers, you would often realize that they are not aware of the brand of their own cupboard.

So, what does a marketer actually do when they meet consumers? The answer is: a marketer deeply tries to understand consumers who are brand agnostic. It's the deeper understanding of the consumer that allows a marketer to build campaigns that make a brand relatable. A marketer doesn't ask why a consumer buys a certain brand, rather the marketer tries to understand the attitudes, beliefs, and behaviour of a consumer with or without the context of a brand or category.

Consumer Immersion

The most important tool for a marketer is to spend time at leisure with consumers or should we just say 'people'. Asking them about their childhood, their day-to-day challenges, thoughts on society and life in general. These deep and meaningful conversations often lead to the most insightful discoveries.

> As marketers, we often meet with consumers
> to build hypothesis and validate our ideas.
> However, most insightful conversations are
> those that are carried out without any
> agenda and are aimed at understanding
> people in general.

A consumer immersion is often a no holds barred conversation where a marketer discusses everything under the sun to know the person (consumer) they wish to understand closely.

The Discussion

While the practice of consumer immersion aims at understanding a consumer, it's useful to have a loose structure to the conversation so that the marketer is able to gain a large breadth of information. The key areas that I try and cover when I meet consumers are usually as follows:

- Childhood memories: In order to understand a person, it's often important to learn about the experiences that shaped their world view. In our childhood, we are most malleable and impressions formed in the early years often play a significant role in shaping our personalities. This is where most of our values are formed.

- Reflections on life: How is the world today different for their kids from the one they grew up in? What has changed; is the change good or bad? This question helps us to further understand the consumer's belief system.

- What is their happiest memory and what didn't make them happy? This, again, adds to the collage of the consumer's life and what they value.

- How do they feel in general about their day-to-day life? Is it hectic or easy? Are they satisfied or dissatisfied with how they live and what would they like to change about their life? At this point, we start getting a sense of how their values and beliefs shape their attitude towards their life.

- A day in life: In this part of the conversation, we try and understand their behaviours, daily rituals, priorities, and what their life is all about.

- Relationships: The role their spouses, children, friends, and family play in their life.

- Only after we have familiarized ourselves with the beliefs, attitudes, and behaviours of the consumers, we try to understand the role that the brand's product category plays in their life. Where do they use it, how often, and why?

- We then try and understand brand's perception through projective techniques. Often the consumer struggles to express how they may view the imagery of a brand. However, when you ask them to associate various brands with celebrities, they are promptly able to do so. For example, Oreo may be seen as trendy brand as it is associated with Indian actor Ranbir Kapoor, while a Good Day biscuit may be seen as a brand that has timeless appeal when the veteran actor Amitabh Bachchan, matching this appeal, endorses it. And a Jim Jam may be associated with the actor Varun Dhawan who is known for his quirkiness and fun element.

The above-mentioned points can serve as a good template for anyone starting out in their pursuit of understanding consumers. However, for an experienced marketer, a good consumer is essentially the one with whom you can have a rich conversation with as you would have with a friend. The aim is to closely understand the person you are spending time with.

Case Studies

Meeting consumers has always been an insightful experience. However, there have been times where consumer immersions have been truly discerning and some of those insights eventually became the base of the consumer insight and our brand concepts.

1. **Cadbury Celebrations:** In 2008, we set out to understand the spirit of Diwali festival among our consumers in tier-I metro cities of Mumbai and Delhi and tier-II cities of Bareilly, Nagpur, and Rajkot. Our aim was to understand how consumers celebrate Diwali and the emotions they associate with the festival. Interestingly, when we met consumers living in a housing society in Mumbai, they

shared that they don't really know their neighbors that well. However, during Diwali, they ensure that everyone in the building has a great time in order to embrace the festive spirit. So, they seek monetary contribution from all the residents of the society, book the society hall, and organize a dinner and fireworks. However, we observed that despite the fun and frolic of celebrating the festival, the depth of emotional connections within the people, strangely, seemed to be missing.

When we travelled further to Bareilly, we spent time with a wonderful family where kids, their parents, and grandparents all lived on the first floor of a duplex, while their landlord lived on the ground floor. We spent an entire day interviewing every member of the family, and later in the evening, we also got to attend a small Diwali party the family threw for their relatives who would usually be present during such festivals.

While the overall experience was immersive, the penny dropped when one of the family members said, "Our kids and the kids of our landlord have been attending school together for the past seven years. Everyone in school believes that they are brothers." This statement stuck with me. We observed that in metro cities, the warmth between relationships has gradually disappeared, but it still exists, to some degree, in smaller towns.

This understanding made us wonder: what if Cadbury Celebrations were to turn the festival of Diwali into a 'National Happiness Break' where we give ourselves the right to truly invest our time in reaching out to our friends, family, and neighbours? This gave birth to the popular campaign—*"Iss Diwali aap kise khush karenge?"*

2. **Gems Surprise:** Around the same time, in 2008, Cadbury was facing an onslaught from Kinder Joy—a unique chocolate that comes with a surprise toy then priced at ₹30. For Cadbury, where 70% of its business still came from ₹5 and ₹10 SKUs, it was a surprise that a consumer today was willing to pay so much for just 20 g of chocolate and an inexpensive toy. So, it was again time for us to go out there and meet consumers.

   Here, we decided to meet homemakers in their 30s and 40s with a young kid at home. Now, given that I had just started my career in brand management, I had my own perceptions—largely coloured by my memories as a child—on how consumers might behave. Now, the initial conversations with these women went as planned. They all recalled their memories of growing up. Most of them shared how their mothers would restrict intake of chips, chocolates, and ice creams giving reasons of being harmful to health, even as they knew that the real reason was that these goodies were considered expensive then and not easy to afford every day. Also, most of these women were brought up in joint families and there was always a mother-in-law in the picture, in whose presence their own mother would don a strict avatar. Life was a little regimented back then and occasions for treats were few and greatly valued.

   However, as society evolved, Indian households became more urban, metropolitan and gradually moved towards being nuclear. The need to stay strict with the children reduced; these homemakers behaved more like friends with their children than as a disciplinarian. Further, affluence grew and knowledge of health and hygiene surfaced. So, suddenly the health worries were those of bad quality water and adulteration in food. Branded snacks then became affordable and trustworthy.

Besides, with the advent of nuclear families, the women had more money at their disposal but less time. Kids became more aware and better negotiators. A small treat to pacify the kids post their shopping visit became a norm and hence a ₹30 chocolate and toy, which would have been prohibitively expensive when they were kids, suddenly became a relevant offer.

Interacting with consumers helps a marketer understand their beliefs, values, and attitudes. This answers why consumers do certain things and helps explain what the marketer observes happening in the market. However, the objective of a consumer immersion is to deeply understand the consumer and their purchase behaviour. While meeting many consumer yield insights, each consumer has unique tastes and choices. Therefore, to make sense of the vast amounts of consumer data, we rely on segmentation which we will cover in the next chapter.

The Marketer's Checklist

- Consumers don't really care about our brand, but possessing an in-depth understanding of consumer behaviour is the key to make our brands relevant to them.

- A great way to understand consumers is to interact with numerous people and try to understand their lives through deep and engaging conversations.
- In these conversations, a skilful marketer is able to understand the attitudes and beliefs of a consumer which eventually has a bearing on their purchase behaviour.
- This deeper understanding of consumers helps us glean consumer insights which form the basis for impactful communications and innovations of activations thereby making our brand endearing to consumers.

SEGMENTATION

I t's now clear that understating the consumer in broad brushes helps a marketer decode trends and build a broad category strategy. However, when it comes to positioning a brand or building a sharp activation plan, one needs to dig a little deeper and understand various clusters consumers can be segmented into.

While it's great to have an offer that works for 'everyone', it is also often a vulnerable strategy which can be attacked by a competing brand that understands the needs of a particular cluster of consumers better. Hence, it's important for a marketer to be able to divide the market into groups that are more homogeneous so that the 'most valuable consumer group' can be found.

Basis of Segmentation

While every human being is unique and can rarely be compared to another, there exists certain characteristics or traits which are shared universally.

Say, most of us may start our alcoholic beverage drinking journey with a beer or a rum and then gradually experiment with whisky once we start working. Similarly, most Indians may purchase a Maruti as their first car followed by a Hyundai as their second.

If we observe these trends closely, we realize that there are certain common consumer characteristics which have a correlation with buying choices. This correlation between consumer segments and buying behaviour forms the bases of segmentation. Understanding the right variables such as age, income, gender, etc., helps a marketer arrive at segments between which a targeting choice can be made.

Types of Segmentation

Segmentation can be done on almost every variable that we can measure about consumers. It is, however, only useful if it directly correlates to the buying behaviour of the consumer category being studied. A few examples where the link is intuitive are as follows:

1. **Income:** Given the large amount to be spent in buying a house and the fact that it is the preferred savings tool for most consumers, it's most directly correlated with affluence. Therefore, in order to segment consumers for property purchases, one is most likely to uncover the annual income of the family as the key segmentation variable.

2. **Age:** Given that chocolates and candies are often considered a treat for kids, the clear segmentation variable that comes to mind here is the age of the

consumer. For instance, brands like Cadbury Gems and sugar-boiled candies are expected to be consumed by kids while brands like Perk, 5 Star, and Munch are expected to be consumed more often by teens while dark chocolate is expected to be preferred by adults.

3. **Gender:** In the case of clothes, the first variable for segmentation is predominantly gender and it's obvious how buying choices and fit of brands would strongly correlate with your dressing style and the second variable would be affluence.

4. **Geography:** Culture of consumers in a particular part of the country is often a powerful segmentation variable where a brand like Lux might be preferred in the northern and eastern states of the country while a brand like Santoor may be popular in Maharashtra, Karnataka, and Andhra Pradesh.

Segmentation Process

The formal process of segmentation follows a statistical technique known as cluster analysis where we are able to plot the correlation between variables and consumption. However, the key principle followed here is that, a listing study is initially conducted and a vast amount of data is collected over a statistically representative sample.

The collected data includes all kinds of demographic variables like age, socio-economic class (SEC), salary, education, region as well as ownership data like having the right white goods, a car, house, etc., and category purchase behaviours like types of brands purchased, how often, and in what quantity.

A skilled marketer now tries to ascertain
patterns between the variables collected
and consumed.

Once a sufficiently strong relationship is found between brand and category choices versus consumer variables, we are ready to cut the data in form or segments.

Segment Cuts

Once the right segmentation variable has been identified, the task of making segments is about clustering the data linked to the segments in question. However, what is interesting at this stage is to also understand how the beliefs, attitudes, and behaviour would be read across these segments. Let me demonstrate this with a hypothetical example.

In the case of automobiles, we arrive at affluence as the key segmentation variable. Going ahead, we may uncover three key segments that a new car manufacturer can evaluate for targeting: (i) annual household income of less than ₹25 lakh, (ii) annual income between ₹25 lakh and ₹50 lakh, and (iii) income above ₹50 lakh. As the marketer dives a little deeper, a more nuanced consumer portrait might emerge.

Income less than ₹25 lakh: The marketer might realize that most car purchasers with an annual household income less than ₹25 lakh tend to be first-time car buyers. Additionally, they may be less than 35 years of age in say 60-70% of the instances. Furthermore, they may rate mileage and affordability as their most important criteria while selecting a car.

Income between ₹25 lakh and ₹50 lakh: Upon deeper investigation, a marketer might realize that most car buyers in this income segment are often buying their second car and are also older in age. They tend to have families with older kids and may look for safety features as one of the key criteria in brand selections.

Income above ₹50 lakh: These car buyers might often be in their forties, working in established firms, and living in mega metros. These car buyers might prefer luxury features found in high-end cars like sedans.

Through this example, we realize that while the right segmentation variable helps us understand how to arrive at the different segments, we might have to do more work to understand these segments in greater detail through a 'consumer portrait'—more on that soon.

Target Consumer Segment

> After the segments have been identified, we must next choose which segment we wish to target. This depends on how attractive each segment is and our ability to win against the existing competition in this segment.

Often, we may choose more than one segment with various offers or initiatives from the stable of brands.

a) **Segment attractiveness:** To understand how attractive a segment is, we look at three parameters:
   - **Size of the segment:** How large the segment is at

present from the perspective of business value of the number of consumers.

- **Growth of the segment:** How fast is the segment growing based on past trends or the potential in the future.
- **Profitability:** How profitable the segment is. Some segments may be large, but would need mass pricing while others may be small but have an opportunity for us to sell at a premium.

These three factors help us plot the various advantages or disadvantages of choosing a particular set of consumers to target.

b) **Ability to win:** However, the real choice of the segment to chase often depends upon our ability to win over a set of consumers. This ability can be determined through a range of factors, however, the most important ones are usually:

- **Current consumer base:** You are most likely to win with your current base of consumers. Hence, if Cadbury has established its penetration with mass market products, a new offer in a similar segment would see faster adoption while something priced similar to Lindt may not.
- **Route to market:** In order to win over a set of consumers, your product or brand must first be available at an arm's reach. Therefore, by studying where a set of consumers shop and plotting your ability to reach them at the stores would have a large bearing on your ability to win them over.

- **Product delivery:** The journey of consumers choosing a brand as their preferred one starts with the first trial and then eventually becomes their regular choice based on how satisfied they are by the delivery that a brand offers.

Hence, an honest evaluation of your internal strengths is crucial in arriving at the target consumer segment. Once this segment is identified, we proceed with the next step which is to build a holistic consumer portrait of our choice of target group.

Target Consumer Segment

The Marketer's Checklist

- Segmentation is the process of uncovering the range of variables which are correlated to consumption or purchase.

- Studying these variables helps us create discrete consumer segments.
- Once segments are identified, we must study how attractive each of the segments are, and where we have the highest ability to win.
- Attractiveness of segments depends upon the size of each segment, how fast it's growing, and how profitable it is likely to be.
- Our 'right to win' depends on various factors, the most important ones being our current penetration in each segment, our ability to reach out to them through right channels, and the ability of our product to deliver to the segment's needs.
- This evaluation helps us arrive at the 'most valuable consumer', following which we proceed with the creation of 'consumer portraits'.
- This then leads us to the understanding of the target consumer segment.

CREATING CONSUMER PORTRAIT

I t's perhaps the passion for understanding people and diverse cultures that has kept me engaged throughout my career. The 'Aha! moment' of discovering unique aspects about the target group is usually an unforgettable experience for most marketers like me.

When I joined Britannia, the first thing I did was to meet and interact with consumers of various products of our portfolio: Good Day, Britannia Marie, 50-50, Treat, Bourbon, and NutriChoice Digestive. I tried to understand which group of consumers each brand talks to. This process of dividing the market into relatively homogeneous clusters is known as segmentation. We then try and go beyond the data and bring these segments to life through a consumer portrait by understanding what drives and motivates them.

Construction of a consumer portrait requires a balance of both—art and science. The scientific component entails the quantitative data (population sample size) that is measured through a listing study. However, the true art (meaningful portion of the exercise) is to go beyond the data and number crunching and look at the qualitative aspects of the study, i.e., observing attitudes, beliefs, and behaviours of the consumers that not only explain the data but also provide wonderful insights into the consumer psyche.

Arriving at the Segments

> As discussed in the previous section, a detailed study, often known as a listing study, collects all measurable data of the consumers. A cluster analysis helps us understand the demographic variables that best explains consumer behaviour.

In case of certain categories, though, the variables may be quite straightforward. For instance, types of chocolates may have a correlation with the age of the consumer or the type of real estate purchased may correlate with family's disposable income. However, for some categories, the correlation may not be so straightforward. An example of such a category may be biscuits where some hypothetical segments could be as follows:

1. Parle-G biscuits for consumers from low-income strata where affordability may make this their preferred choice of category.
2. Consumers from younger age groups may have a strong correlation with the consumption of cream biscuits.
3. Homemakers of a broader income segment may be the biggest consumers of Britannia Marie, while the consumption of Digestive biscuits may be higher in older men.

4. Cream Crackers and Rusk may find a large number of consumption in the segments of older men or those with health challenges.
5. Cookies may be more popular towards middle-income families.

As we can see, consumer segments are often a combination of a number of segmentation variables, including (but not restricted to) age, income levels, educations, gender, and health. The first phase of the construction of the consumer portrait, however, is about putting together of all data available on the consumer.

Plotting the Segment Behaviour

After segments have been identified, the marketer is then able to organize the data that yields a deeper understanding of how each of the segments behave. Say in the case of fruit juices, we realize that three distinct clusters emerge which have a direct correlation to consumer's purchase and consumption behaviour. The key segmentation variable being the age of the target audience.

1. Mothers of kids below the age of 18 years.
2. Teens and young adults between 18 and 30 years.
3. Adults above the age of 30 years.

We will now try to understand these three clusters in further detail.

Data may reveal that choice in juices for mothers of kids below the age of 18 years is driven by taste and flavour.

They might prefer buying small packs and have household consumption primarily during the evenings.

While in the case of teens and young adults, the data we investigate may show that most of the consumption happens in the mornings and mid-mornings. They may prefer large packs of expensive juices like RAW Pressery which provide explicit health benefits.

In case of adults over the age of 30, we may realize that they primarily buy affordable large packs of 1 litre and hunt for bargains in supermarkets (for e.g., Buy 1+1 Free offer) and often buy during the festive season when discounts are offered on a large scale.

All of the above data may provide quantitative understanding of the consumers, however, the real task of a marketer starts with the analyzing the qualitative data which reveals the true consumer psyche.

Understanding the Segments

> After plotting the key segment characteristics, marketers now try to gain a deeper understanding into the consumers' beliefs, attitudes, and behaviours through qualitative research. This involves meeting and interacting with a large number of consumers in groups and getting to know them in depth.

The three attributes of consumers are beliefs, attitudes, and behaviours. Let's try to understand them in detail as a marketer.

- **Beliefs:** Beliefs shape our perception and play out in category choices. For e.g., people who have always believed in herbal or traditional medicine, often buy herbal-based products, and so on.
- **Attitudes:** They are shaped by how we respond to stimulus in our daily lives. A generation ago, when money was scarce, we might have a positive disposition towards homemade food, street food, etc. However, the youth today may have a positive attitude towards organic products, new-age superfoods, and so on.
- **Behaviours:** These are shaped by our beliefs and attitudes. An in-depth understanding of attitudes and beliefs helps explain real behaviours in terms of how we live our daily lives and shape our lifestyle choices.

Taking forward the same hypothetical example of juices from the previous section, the understanding of consumer behaviour may reveal several aspects:

1. **Mothers of kids below the age of 18 years:** Here, we may realize that she believes that parenting today is tough as kids have become smarter than their previous generation and there is a need to constantly negotiate with them. She is able to offer juice to her child as a more nutritious option as against aerated drinks in the evening and hence her choice of juice is driven by taste and flavours that her kid would enjoy.
2. **Teens and young adults between the ages of 18 to 30 years:** In their case, we may realize that social media has helped them belong to a progressive world where they are aware of international trends. The look for new

and exciting food choices that are extremely healthy yet wholesome and delicious.

3. **Adults above the age of 30:** However, in their case, we may find that somewhat traditional values persist and most of their juice purchases are a way of flaunting their status, especially during family gatherings, get-togethers, and festivals. Hence, they look for bargains to balance their budget yet look good in front of their friends and relatives.

Hence, this qualitative understanding of consumers helps us move a bit deeper from 'what' is being observed to 'why' is it really happening.

The Consumer Portrait

> The process of understanding the consumer offers us the choice of three distinct segments to target with different triggers and barriers. This detailed understanding of the consumers, agnostic of any category, helps us build distinct consumer portraits and makes our targeting choices.

Taking forward the above example, the three 'consumer portraits' that may emerge are:

1. **The smart negotiator:** The mother of kids who believes she is smart and savvy and makes discerning choices for her and her family. She believes that juices are healthy and looks for delightful tasting juices with rich flavours

to surprise and please her family with a healthy and tasty choice.

2. **The health buddy:** Is a health-conscious individual between 18 and 30 years who believes that their choices have the power to make them feel confident about their looks and style. They purchase tasty and international fruit juice packs as they believe that they deserve to consume the best products available in the market.

3. **The status seeker:** Is a traditional bargain hunter of above 30 years of age, driven by the social need of looking good and being accepted among peers and family. This individual looks for safe and secure choices befitting their stature while entertaining their friends and family.

	Smart Negotiator	**Healthy Buddy**	**Status Seeker**
Beliefs	Parenting is tough and I need to negotiate with my kids	Social media has helped me uncover global trends	Retain traditional values and be a conscious consumer
Attitude	Seek a win-win with my kids	I make progressive choices	Seek to make choices that express my status
Behaviour	Offer juice to my kids as a healthy and tasty snack	Drink healthy juices as a part of holistic lifestyle	Offer juices to guests to reflect my status

This table of the target segments helps a marketer in making choices on whom to target. Other metrics like how large these segments are and how easy or difficult is it for a marketer to win these consumers over eventually helps in making the targeting choice.

Once a marketer is able to plot the right cut of segments, it's now their task to understand the consumer deeper, first through the quantitative data and then through the qualitative research. A combination of these two leads to the consumer portrait which is an evocative description of the most-valued consumer and the one that a brand must eventually tailor their marketing mix towards.

The Marketer's Checklist

- Segmentation starts by dividing the market into relatively homogeneous clusters of consumers.
- This is done by first collecting data about the consumers through a listing study and then conducting cluster analysis to see how details of the consumers correlate to their consumption patterns.
- After clusters have been identified, the marketer needs to understand why a cluster behaves in a particular manner.
- Some of the conclusions may be straightforward, like a low-income household may purchase affordable biscuits.
- An insight usually emerges from a deeper understanding of the consumer, say a housewife may see herself as a smart negotiator or an early jobber may want to achieve a particular high status through their choices.
- This is how an in-depth understanding of the beliefs, attitudes, and behaviours of consumers is known and a consumer portrait is built.

UNCOVERING CONSUMER INSIGHT

Once the 'most valuable consumer segment' has been found, we can move towards the next phase of the consumer journey which is to find 'consumer insight'. As you must have realized by now, a marketer moves from a broad understanding of the consumer to creation of a consumer portrait of the chosen segment. And once a detailed understanding of the 'target group' has been gathered, we move on to learn about the consumer insight which essentially helps us understand how to position our brand in order to deliver business growth.

Why is an Insight Required

Before we proceed with the understanding of consumer insights, it's important to know why these are so precious to marketers and why do we spend so much time mining them.

An insight is essentially the backbone of a concept or the reason why consumers value the products and services we market. It is actually an understanding of a consumer's life that makes our products or services relevant to them.

To give you an example: Santoor has built its relevance over the years as a brand that promises to make your skin look younger. This is based on the insight that most women do not wish to be defined by their age. It's this need to look and feel younger that makes Santoor's proposition relevant and worth investing into till date.

An insight is, therefore, a perceptive understanding of consumers that has the power to create opportunities for business growth.

Building the Mind Map

The first step towards uncovering meaningful insights is to build a mind map of your consumers. A mind map is often created when the marketing and the creative agency form a team of around eight to ten people who spend four to six weeks with consumers and try to closely observe everything about them. Each team member is expected to bring at least 50 individual observations.

Also, at this stage, a broad cross-section of consumers are identified:

- The first, being the most-valued consumer segment, say are teens or housewives as the case may be.
- Experts who are expected to know a lot about the target group. For instance, teachers or pediatricians in the case of children, or parlour owners in case of a cosmetics brand.
- And outliers—for e.g., someone who has never used cosmetics. This helps us understand barriers.

After which the teams divide themselves in groups of twos and threes to go out there and talk to consumers, interview them, or, in some cases, even live with them for a couple of days.

Here are a few interesting examples: A brand manager of Axe deodorant wants to understand their most valuable consumer segment—most probably young adults in their 20s pursuing their college degrees and living in a hostel. In this case, a brand team may even decide to spend a few weekends living with these potential consumers in their hostels, participate in their weekend rituals, and closely try to observe and understand everything they do.

In the same way, if a brand manager of shampoo sachets wishes to understand the lives of specific consumers with a monthly income of a few thousand rupees, again, the team can visit the consumers at their homes and even share a few meals which would allow them the access and and help them gain a perspective on their lives.

Moreover, the teams also go through all the available content on the target group, say in the form of previous research material, reports, news articles, etc. In some cases, accompanying the target group during their shopping visits and observing their actions of buying or interacting with the category can also be extremely useful. For instance, simply watching the target group interact with jewelers in a shop can be extremely insightful.

As the teams spend time with consumers, they note their observations on simple post-it notes. The process is to strictly note only the actual behaviour of the consumers. At this point, there is no role of interpretation. The teams specifically note only that they see, hear, or read about the consumers.

Connecting the Dots

Once a large number of observations—typically between 300 and 500 contributed by the entire team—are collected, the team then gathers in a conference room for a 'connect' session where all these observations are pasted over the walls of the room and discussed.

> This allows us to peer into the consumers' minds by placing on the walls every and any observation the team members may have found interesting or worth noting down.

Next, the team members again divide themselves in groups of twos and threes and create clusters of similar sounding observations. Say one member of a group might like an observation that says: 'Mothers are often worried if their children aren't eating well'. Other group members would try and scan the walls for other observations that belong to the same cluster. Some examples of observations that may ring similar could be 'mothers insist that their kids must drink a glass of milk every day' or 'kids are happy to eat junk food, but when it comes to their meals, they keep leftovers on the plate', and so on.

The aim is to clear the walls and collate everything that has been observed into say 20-30 stacks of 20 observations each. This helps us arrive at 20-30 such clusters of thoughts that dominate the mind of the target group.

Mining the Insight

The next phase of the consumer journey requires the most skill and this is the portion where the time spent with the consumer comes in handy. Here, the groups either sit together or separately and start interrogating the clusters to understand what's really going on. This part of the consumer journey is called the '5 Whys' as the task is to ask 'why' at least five times to dive deeper into the mind of the consumer.

For instance, we have come across a cluster of observations where we realize that the youth feel that life is extremely busy, and they have a lot to do. We may also find that, in today's world, they feel that there are enough opportunities to chase their passions and also earn a reasonable standard of living. When we interrogate this space, we may realize that the reasons why the youth today feels this way is because of the rise of popular culture fanned by shows like 'Shark Tank India' aired on OTT platforms where they show how several young people today are achieving success and venturing into entrepreneurship.

As we dive in deeper, we may realize that today's youth doesn't want to miss out on these opportunities and is trying to find easy hacks of getting ahead. They may feel that there are smarter ways to achieve progress rather than the old-fashioned ones or walking a straight path. However, as the groups and team members bring back the conversations that they observed and the thoughts that they witnessed, the insight that we discover could address very different opportunities.

This same observation of the state of the youth may have led Nescafé to the insight relevant for Nescafé's *'Badal Life ki Raftaar'* advertisement which talks about the fact that the youth today is seeking partners in their journey of wanting to maximize their life's opportunities.

On the other hand, the same insight led 5 Star to come up with #Eat5StarDoNothing Ad which depicts that today's youth—who are always on their toes and undergo a lot of pressure in their pursuit to succeed in life—can normalize the act of relaxing. They could forget all the stress and enjoy that pleasurable moment of doing nothing by simply eating a bar of 5 star chocolate.

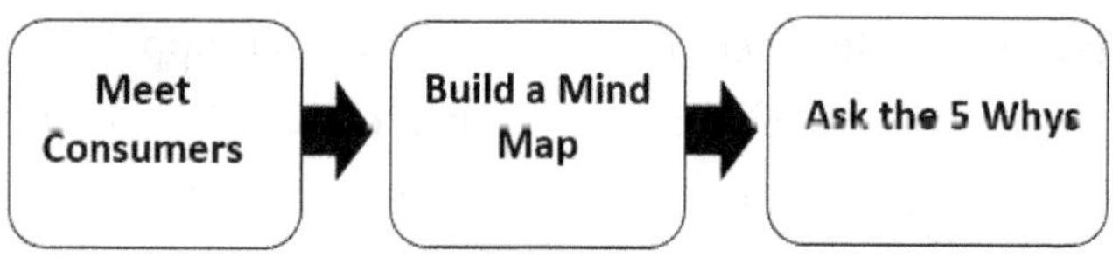

However, towards the end of the insight mining process, the task that the team needs to accomplish is to arrive at unique ideas that they have understood about the life of their target group that explains the observed behaviour as captured in their post-it notes. In the next section, we will cover how a marketer moves from the consumer insight to the concept card that brings alive the opportunity for the brand to activate through innovation, communication, or activation.

The Marketer's Checklist

- An insight is a perceptive understanding of your consumers that has the power to create opportunities for business growth.
- In order to uncover the consumer insight, we must first create a mind map of the consumer which is done through a team of people who note down all observations of interest.
- Observations are made based on real behaviour which is seen, heard, or read. There is no aspect of interpretation at this stage.
- Once 300 to 500 observations are captured, marketers search for similar patterns in those observations and then try and understand why those patterns exist.
- These patterns are then examined through the lens of '5 Whys' which help us arrive at a universal consumer truth on which the brand may be positioned.

BRAND CONCEPT

The brand concept is where the rubber meets the road. The process so far is quite theoretical and linked to understanding consumers. However, when it comes to brand concept, we can start visualizing how we will activate a consumer opportunity. Hence, the brand concept is perhaps the most important document that a marketer creates. It contains the essence of the brand. It starts with: why a consumer should be interested in the offer and then answers why the offer is best placed to resolve the consumer tension and ends with a compelling reason to believe which helps seal the deal.

The insight begins with the consumer insight and then links the product through a series of steps which we shall now discuss in subsequent segments.

The Consumer Insight

As we discussed in the previous chapter, the key for any product or services to find a compelling role in the life of a consumer is to always begin with what the consumer is thinking or feeling. A deeper understanding of the consumer is then noted in the form of 'consumer insight' which usually captures a natural tension (explained in the examples below) that a brand or service can try and provide a solution for.

> The consumer insight usually refers to gaining a deeper understanding of the world view of a consumer. It starts with the life of the consumer and not the product or services.

Furthermore, insights are usually crafted in a first-person perspective so that they best articulate the opportunity or challenge from that perspective.

A few examples of powerful insights that have led to several different consumer opportunities are as follows:

1. "I wish I could find nutritious snacks that my kids also find tasty!"

   This universal insight is the basis of several new categories like packaged juices, value-added dairy products like milkshakes, cheese, and flavoured yogurts as well as breakfast cereals like Kellogg's Chocos.

2. "Today, I feel like a partner in my child's progress rather than a disciplinarian like my mother was with me!"

   This insight has led to powerful brand campaigns such Surf Excel's 'Daag Achhe Hain', or a Kinder Joy's little treats. It's has also been leveraged by brands like Britannia Milk Bikis in Tamil Nadu.

3. And then there is the universal insight: "Happiness spreads when shared!"

   This insight has been the bedrock of the world's most powerful brand campaigns of Cadbury, Coca Cola, Domino's, and many more.

The Offer

Once we identify a compelling consumer insight, we then link it with the product or service—this is the core of brand positioning.

> The offer must be presented in a manner that it specifically links to the problem or consumer tension that the insight has helped uncover.

While Coca Cola might be a brand that encourages you to 'Open Happiness' in a refreshing bottle or Cadbury Dairy Milk may be the modern *'meetha'* that celebrates moments of goodness with ads such as *'Kuch Achha Ho Jaaye, Kuch Meetha Ho Jaaye'*, this brand positioning only makes sense when it ties back to something fundamental that the consumer is seeking.

To reiterate, while an insight is usually universal, the 'product offer' is quite specific and is built on the basis of certain specific 'benefits' which the product or service in question can convincingly deliver.

The Benefit

The next level of brand concept is a sharp articulation of the precise benefit that the offer delivers to the consumer. While the offer is often emotional in nature, the benefit is usually functional and is linked to what makes the brand in question authentically own this positioning.

So, in the case of Cadbury, the fact that its taste is considered as the gold standard among the other chocolates in India for several decades and has been associated with moments of celebration both large and small over the life spans of many generations give it the credibility to deliver its positioning as the modern-day *meetha* for Indians.

Similarly, dairy products like milkshakes, cheese, and yogurts—made with the goodness of pure milk—often lend credibility in being able to promise an offer that balances nutrition and taste for families.

While the offer or brand positioning is often unique, the benefit might become a little more generic and replicable. It is here that the 'reason to believe' comes to the rescue and lends credibility.

Reason to Believe

A reason to believe is often crucial in enabling brands to own a long-term differentiation in their benefits. A cheese brand positioned on health may look at vitamin and mineral fortification to buttress its claim as being truly healthy. A parent may be generally aware that cheese is healthy as it's made of milk, a clear nutritional claim on the front of the pack mentioning the vitamin and mineral fortification often lends greater authenticity and credibility to the claim.

The iconic image of two glasses pouring milk on Dairy Milk chocolate—which the brand has carried over several decades—has become a marker of quality and hence buttresses its credibility as the gold standard of chocolate.

Positioning

After the insight generation process, the brand team may arrive at several competing concepts—all of which may seem equally compelling. It is now that we must view the concepts from the context of our competition and examine which ones are most likely to win in the market.

The three factors which help us choose the winning concept are as follows:

a) **Compelling to the consumer:** The brand concept must successfully solve a large and meaningful need-gap in the consumer's life. Many a time when the gap is large or similar to the delivery of the category, we may have many brands sitting on the same benefit with limited differentiation

   An example of this is the need to feel glamorous after using a bathing bar. Brands such as Lux, Santoor, Rexona, and Godrej No. 1, thus, operate in spaces very close to each other.

b) **Differentiated from the competition:** This is then the next most important criterion. How does a brand differentiate itself from the competition? Lux uses exotic ingredients and fragrances as well as consistent Bollywood tie-ups to differentiate itself. Santoor, on the other hand, uses a singular benefit of younger-looking skin to sharpen their positioning as distinct from Lux.

c) **Uniquely deliverable by us:** While a brand concept helps the brand to stand out from the competition, the product often needs a unique 'reason to believe'—to make the differentiation credible. And, hence, the consistent messaging of sandal and turmeric in Santoor helps it retain its positioning.

Furthermore, it's very important to choose a positioning which is not easy for the competition to emulate. Therefore, it's important to be aware of technology or intellectual property rights and law that can help protect the brand to hold its positioning over time in case of any disputes with the competitors.

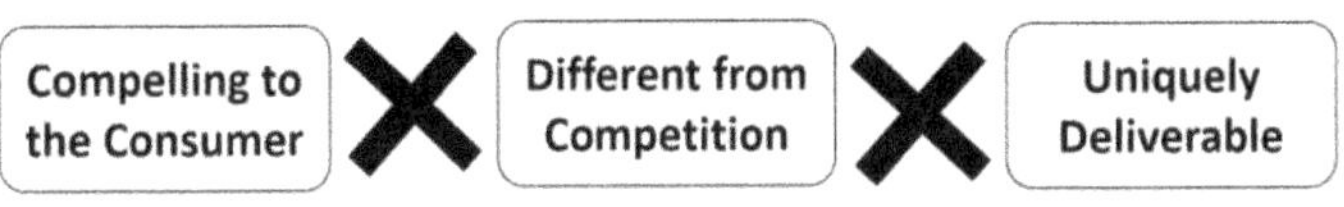

The Marketer's Checklist

- A brand concept begins with consumer insight and then links the brand offer or its positioning as the solution for the consumer tension that the consumer is seeking to resolve.
- The brand offer is often emotional in nature and supported by functional delivery that acts as the benefit that the consumer derives.
- The 'reason to believe' lends credibility to the offer and helps provide a long-term point of differentiation that facilitates building a compelling brand.
- The brand concept is the key to successful brand positioning. We must, therefore, evaluate the strength of the concept versus competition as we choose the concept for brands.

- When taken in together, all these components mentioned above build a strong core of the brand that can further be activated through advertising.

3

ACTIVATING THE BRAND

How Are Advertisements Made
How to Deliver Winning Activation
Events, Public Relations, and Word of Mouth
The Logic of Consumer Promotions
Use of Celebrities in Marketing
Making the Media Plan

HOW ARE ADVERTISEMENTS MADE

Nothing excites budding marketers more than the idea of making eye-catching advertisements. But ever given a thought on how is it actually done? It is more of an art than science; something that the creative wizards and geniuses at the advertising agency pull out of their magic hat.

However, there is also a definite science behind how it's all done. So, let's understand the art and science behind a winning brand advertisement.

Making an advertisement entails a few basic steps:

1. Figuring out the core issue
2. Understanding your consumer
3. Uncovering the insight
4. Making the creative

Figuring Out the Core Issue

The most critical thing to do before kicking off any creative process is to obtain crystal clarity on the brand task you are trying to work on.

When I was working on Cadbury Gems' *'Raho Umarless'* campaign, our 'brand task' was to make Gems the 'brand for me' for kids and teens, as our kiddy advertising always made Gems come across as 'the brand for my younger sibling'.

Similarly, for Cadbury Celebrations' *'Toh Iss Diwali Aap Kise Khush Karenge?'* campaign, we wanted to make 'aware non-purchasers', who were aware of the brand but didn't think about buying it, to think about it during their purchase occasions.

So, getting precise clarity on what you are working on and trying to resolve is the first step.

Understanding the Consumer

The next step, perhaps, is the most exciting one for any marketer because it is best executed through a workshop. Here, you first gather the team — comprising brand manager, consumer insights manager, R&D manager, sales manager, agency planner, agency client servicing, design teams, etc., — into a conference room and then you break into groups of twos and threes each and head out to meet consumers and conduct in-depth interviews. This should be backed with thorough research of your consumers.

> Throughout these visits and interactions with consumers, you must jot down your observations. At this stage, though, it's critical to write 'pure observations' based on what you are watching, hearing, or reading and not include your guesses as to 'why' the consumer is behaving in that manner.

Finally, each team member brings around 50 observations on post-it notes and pastes them on the walls of a large conference room. A total of around 500 observations (post-it notes) gathered from all the team members adorning the walls of the conference room then form the 'mind map' of your consumer. Everything you know about your consumer is on those walls.

Next, you club similar sounding observations to get a larger picture of your consumer's behavioural pattern of what you observed as a group.

After you have uncovered the 'what' of the consumer, you start debating the 'why', what's really at the heart of what you are observing. You then ask 'why?' at least five times to reach an Insight—as discussed in the previous chapter.

Uncovering the Insight

The whole process is truly intriguing. It's amazing that when I carried out this process in India, Nepal, and Dubai, I observed completely different behaviours.

I realized that the consumers in India are so caught up in their passionate pursuit towards progress that our societies are becoming increasingly insular. This was basically the insight that led Cadbury to come up with *'Toh Iss Diwali App Kisse Khush Karenge'* TV commercial. Similarly, armed with the same insight, Good Day created the 'Smile More for Good Day!' TV commercial with Indian film actor Deepika Padukone highlighting the fact that as Indians we rarely smile at our neighbours.

Interestingly, when I met consumers in Nepal, I realized

that the Nepalese truly believe in every day goodness, contributing to charity, and helping out at old age homes. This is because the country has experienced extreme trauma over the years, especially due to the earthquake recurrences.

On the other hand, I noticed that, in Dubai, the insight used was similar yet different in its own way. The expat communities of Indians, Bangladeshis, Pakistanis, Filipinos felt lonely in an alien country and wished to celebrate the togetherness of their cohorts.

Similarly, while Good Day may always talk about moments of happiness, in India 'happiness' may be found in the moments where you catch up with your neighbours, in Nepal it may mean contributing to society, and for Asians in Dubai it may mean searching for a sense of belonging.

Making the Creative

Once you have gained clarity on the mass consumer behaviour and an insight that is powerful enough to base your communication on, there are three important questions that you need to answer before the creative team can start showing up with scripts.

The first question is 'Who am I?', or what is the way you wish to position your product. An example of a few brilliant campaigns that pulled this off extremely well are Cadbury Dairy Milk which positions chocolates into a 'modern-day meetha' and hence wherever *mithai* is relevant, Cadbury Dairy Milk is too. Coca Cola did this with their *'Thanda Matlab Coca Cola'* TV commercial, where they simply told the consumer that Coke is not just a fancy American beverage, it's also your local roadside *thanda*! So, why have *nimbu pani* (lemon water) when you can reach out for a Coke.

The next important question is: "Why should you buy me?". One of the brands that have done a fabulous job of creatively answering this question is Domino's, because what other tasty and delightful meal can you get under 30 minutes? Axe Deodorant did it equally well by saying that it can make you smell like a candy (alluring) for the opposite sex!

> Finally, the third question is 'How do I make you feel?' The real currency of advertisements is the strong emotions they manage to evoke. This is perhaps the most important question of all!

Does that ad make you feel effervescent and joyful like a can of Coke and do you choose to buy happiness? Or, does it reassure you like an insurance player or does it just make you nostalgic like Paper Boat?

To sum up, while advertising indeed feels magical and has the power to impact people and society at large, the process of creating advertisements is a clear science and starts with possessing crystal clarity of what your core issue is. You then interact with consumers and uncover winning insights. These insights then form the bedrock of your brand concept or creative briefing. Once this is done, the creative hats at the ad agency help you declutter and break down what you want to say when it comes to these three simple questions 'Who am I?', 'Why should you buy me?' and 'How do I make you feel?'. This process could even result in the creation of award-winning ads and, more importantly, these ads deliver business results!

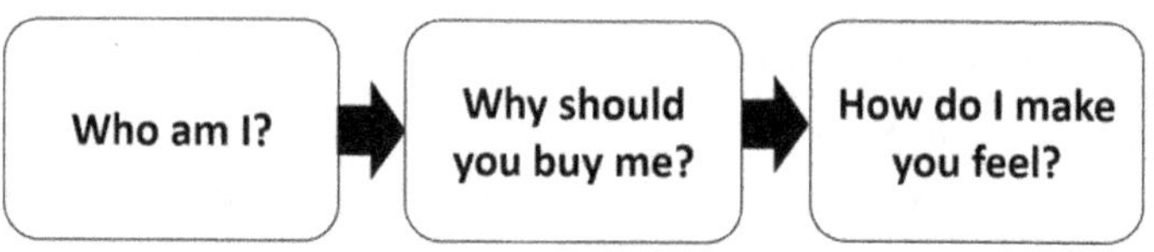

The Marketer's Checklist

- Advertising is often the culmination of the entire process from identification of the core issue to landing the creative solution.
- Marketers and agency partners work closely in understanding the consumer and making of the brand concept. Detailed understanding of the consumer is the key in making an insightful ad creative.
- Interestingly, large global brands own positioning platforms which offer slight flexibility in different markets based on local nuances.
- It's critical for an ad creative to move the consumer from 'Who am I?' to 'Why should you buy me?' by delivering on 'How do I make you feel?'.

HOW TO DELIVER WINNING ACTIVATION

Advertising is the one aspect of marketing that most of us are familiar with, however, often the most powerful tools of behaviour change are 'activations'. While activation is a broader term and is often used to describe everything from advertising to promotions, for the purpose of this section, we shall stick to a specific type of activations which is often called 'experiential activations'.

> Experiential activations are a powerful tool of driving behavioural change as they literally allow consumers to 'experience' the proposition.

Hence, in order to roll out an exciting 'experiential' activation campaign, a marketer must begin with providing the right brief to the agency.

The Activation Brief

An activation brief first asks you to define your 'target consumer' and then seeks answers to four specific questions:

1. What is the current behaviour of the consumers you wish to target?
2. What are consumers currently thinking and what are the possible barriers you may face or the opportunities that you may want to leverage?
3. What is the change in their belief system that you are seeking to make that will help drive further change in consumer behaviour?
4. What will the consumer's behaviour change to?

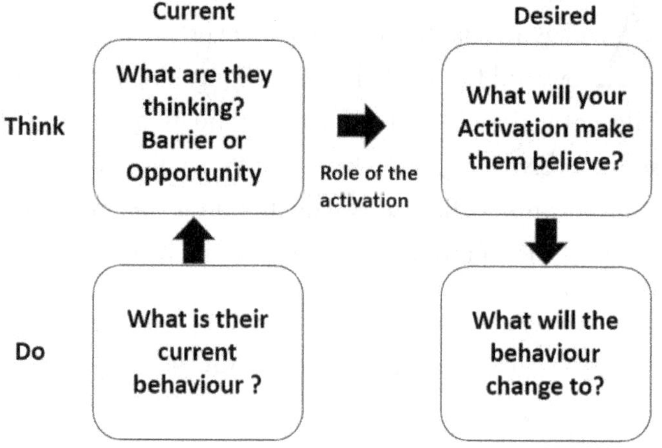

Let's now explore a few different activation tasks with some examples.

Drive Category Relevance

Often for large brands which hold a dominant position in the category, bringing back relevance for the category itself can be a huge activation opportunity. Let me demonstrate this with a few examples.

Assume you work for the popular food aggregator Swiggy and you realize that consumers are still worried about COVID-19 and have been resisting to order food from outside owing to hygiene concerns. In this case, you can clearly articulate the answers to the four questions as follows:

1. I am targeting consumers who have been frequent Swiggy users, but are currently not ordering.
2. The key barrier is that they feel ordering from outside is unsafe.
3. The change in belief that we wish to drive is by stoking their confidence that it's now safe to order.
4. The change in behaviour would be: consumers resume ordering from the app.

Now, this appears fairly intuitive, but it's the act of answering these questions that leads to the activation idea. Some of the activation ideas that may emerge from this example are as follows:

1. Provide an assurance that Swiggy is following all possible safety protocols. One interesting way of doing that is to create a website that features actual live webcam footage of kitchens of their partner restaurants that any user can log on to. The footage will be able to attest and reassure the consumers that safety protocols are being followed.
2. Often the change in behaviour can be driven by creating a belief that if others are doing it (ordering from the app), maybe I am safe to do it as well. This can also be done by celebrating consumers who have already started ordering through a digital campaign.
3. Third idea could be to just bombard fence-sitters with

lucrative promos of 50-75% rebate to spur usage. If a consumer tries it once, he may feel more comfortable the next time.

However, it is crucial to note that if a brand decides to create relevance for the whole category, it talks to non-users as well and addresses barriers.

Drive Competitive Shift

This is perhaps the most common activation brief where you are specifically targeting users of competition brands. One brilliant example here would be The Pepsi Challenge. In the late 70s, through this blind taste challenge, Pepsi found out that the Coke users preferred a more sugary formula in their drinks.

This essentially challenged the consumer belief that Coke is the gold standard of taste and shifted a lot of its market share in the US at that time.

However, there are several such taste or quality challenges that have been run by brands throughout the history of consumer products. The most recent ATL (Above The Line) campaign of the same has been the Sebamed pH 5.5 challenge to conventional soaps like Lux, and Dove where they claim to demonstrate superiority through a chemically-proven formulation.

However, there can also be other interesting activation briefs.

Enhance Imagery Reward Loyalty

Some of the most exciting activations in recent years include Cadbury Dairy Milk Madbury Chocolate Bars where users were asked to suggest their own version or flavour of Cadbury Dairy Milk and the brand, in fact, launched some of the submissions. Such activations are extremely effective when a legacy brand witnesses a drop in imagery scores and its loyal users shift to other brands. These activations reward loyal users and drive retention of the current franchise.

Another powerful campaign which achieved this was the 2009 'Me and Meri Maggi' campaign that rewarded loyalty of the consumers through the tool of nostalgia. According to a case study on Nestlé's Maggi published in *Coursehero. com*, the said campaign was launched to celebrate 25 years of Maggi's presence in India. The idea being that children who had grown up with Maggi as regular food are now adults and many had unique stories to tell. The campaign was a resounding success with over 40,000 stories submitted by devoted Maggi consumers. The 50 best stories were printed on Maggi packaging. More details of this campaign can be found online on the website www.coursehero.com. Here's the link: (https://www.coursehero.com/file/p4aup57/Me-and-Meri-Maggi-In-2009-Nestl%C3%A9-India-launched-the-highly-successful-Me-and/)

Seed Proposition

However, undoubtedly the most powerful activations are those that strengthen the brand proposition and a few compelling examples are:

1. **Britannia Marie Gold My Startup Contest:** This is the example of a campaign which takes forward the promise of the brand of truly understanding the dreams and aspirations of homemakers and proving them an opportunity to do more for themselves by providing seed capital for their start-up idea.

2. **Saffola World Heart Day:** This has been one of the most successful examples of a brand built primarily through the activation of the 'World Heart Day'. This bolstered the confidence among consumers that the brand truly cares about healthy heart.

In an increasingly cluttered and overexposed world, activations bring credibility to a brand as they allow a consumer to experience the brand's point of view. This is extremely effective in the short term, and if done consistently, in the long term as well to drive positive behaviour change in consumers.

The Marketer's Checklist

- Along with advertising and promotions, activation is also a tool of driving behaviour change.
- While advertising drives behaviour change through communication, promotions drive the change by proving brand's value, and activations do the same by curating experiences.
- In order to deliver compelling activations, it's important to start with the right activation brief which links the

current beliefs of the consumers to the behaviour change which you wish to drive.

- Activations can be crafted for several tasks, including building category relevance, driving competitive shift, enhancing imagery, and seeding propositions.

EVENTS, PUBLIC RELATIONS, AND WORD OF MOUTH

Brands create a buzz when they do something noteworthy or have something to talk about. Advertising, activations, and consumer promotions are often considered as the primary levers of the communication strategy. While events, public relations (PR), and word of mouth are quite useful in the creating a certain buzz around the brand. To explain further, a standard communication approach offers passive messages to the consumer and buzz marketing inculcates conversation that leads to customer stickiness and loyalty.

Buzz marketing is also a way for a brand to express its purpose or point of view to its consumers. It is about generating interest and building loyalty, and is often used alongside a regular campaign to enable the audience to participate in the brand's proposition and understand it better.

Opportunities for Buzz Creation

> One must plan for 'buzz creation' ahead
> of time, usually when a new proposition or
> advertisement is being launched or when
> there is an important time of the year and
> the brand wishes to remain in consumer's
> top-of-mind awareness.

Let's discuss a few cases where 'buzz marketing' would be useful and how the brand team would go about planning for the same:

1. **Leveraging a calendar occasion:** A few big purchase and consumption occasions around the year are Valentine's Day, Christmas, Diwali, and Mother's Day. These days are ideal for buzz creation among consumers who have their minds occupied by that particular event. This, therefore, offers great opportunities for brands to engage with the consumers.

2. **Creation of a purpose-led day:** Many of us know Saffola's Brand proposition simply due to their activations on World Heart Day. Did you know that 'Earth Hour', the one hour when we switch off our lights, was actually a brand campaign from an NGO wanting to raise awareness on the environment?

3. **Launch of a new brand or proposition:** This is usually the most common reason of a brand wanting to create buzz and one such incident that comes to my mind is when Richard Branson visited India for the launch of Virgin Telecom.

As you must have now realized, all these events deploy the elements of buzz creation (namely events and PR); this eventually leads to brand's 'word of mouth' publicity. Now, let's explore how a marketer would build a plan for these three examples.

Leveraging a Calendar Occasion

The advantage of this opportunity is that there already exists a lot of conversation among consumers as a build-up to this particular day or date. This helps the brands to express their unique point of view. Let me now share a few interesting examples that have done this well.

One fantastic example would be Cadbury 5 Star's Valentine's Day campaign of 2022 (Valentine's Day Alibi) where they essentially found a quirky insight in the life of their target group, the youth (primarily the singles) who feel uncomfortable on being asked 'What's the plan for the evening?' on Valentine's Day. The brand claims to have created a perfect 'alibi' for these consumers. They further claim that they have taken over an island and renamed it as 'My Cousin's Wedding' so the single youth don't have to lie or feel awkward whenever someone asks them the question. The brand also created television ads and presented on-pack promotions to leverage the same. The chocolate bar wraps had quirky phrases like 'Escape Cheesy Gifts' and a QR code which the consumer could scan and win an escape from Valentine's Day.

Now, while the advertising and promotions are conventional media choices, what is buzzworthy about this example is the outrageousness of the idea that is sure to create conversation amongst their target group for a long time to come.

Creating a Purpose-Led Day

An interesting example of a brand that did this well would be Mama Earth that owned the 'Earth Day' through a 'Goodness Report Card'.

Mama Earth made an endearing video where they got a child to rate them on their environment-friendly initiatives to make the world a better place. The child assesses how the brand has positively impacted the environment by planting 1,00,000 trees, providing safe products without 1,193 toxins, recycling 1,135 tons of plastic, zero animal testing, distributing hand sanitizers and masks, and grades them accordingly.

Such initiatives usually need to be backed up with credible evidence and can be strong tools to lend credibility to a brand's purpose through demonstration of acts beyond just advertising.

Launch of a New Brand or Proposition

One of the greats who always made the most of such opportunities was Steve Jobs, former CEO of Apple. He would build secrecy and mystery around the product and add spectacular effects to dramatize the launch of a new product.

In recent years, Bhavish Aggarwal, CEO of Ola Cabs, used a similar tactic during the launch of homegrown electric scooters from Ola Electric. He did it in style through a fabulous 20-minute video which has garnered over four million views to date. The video begins with Bhavish highlighting adverse impacts of climate change induced by humans and what can be done to reverse it in the backdrop of the massive Ola Futurefactory. He goes on to present how Ola Electric Scooters can be one possible solution sharing the intricate details of the product's each feature that distinguishes it as path-breaking.

The Ground Rules

> Buzz marketing or word-of-mouth marketing engages or moves the consumer through a conversation that is noteworthy or of interest to the consumer. It goes beyond bland communication of a product's features or benefits and instead tries to draw the consumer into the conversation through topics that the consumer can deeply relate to.

Some of the ways in which brands follow this are:

1. **Positioning themselves as an expert**: A commissioned study that can map consumers' perception can often lead to a brand positioning itself as an expert on the topic.
2. **Drama, outrage, or surprise**: These are great ways of drawing consumers' attention and these can be done through an online or offline event.
3. **Organizing large events**: With or without celebrities, these events can grab eyeballs and get consumers talking about the event as well as the brand.

4. **Secret and intrigue:** Building mystery surrounding the brand followed by a grand unveil is also a great way of capturing consumers' attention. This often requires a lot of pre-launch buzz to create a splash.

5. **Acts matter:** If a brand wishes to be noticed, they have to usually rely on some concrete actions which can then be covered by its PR team.

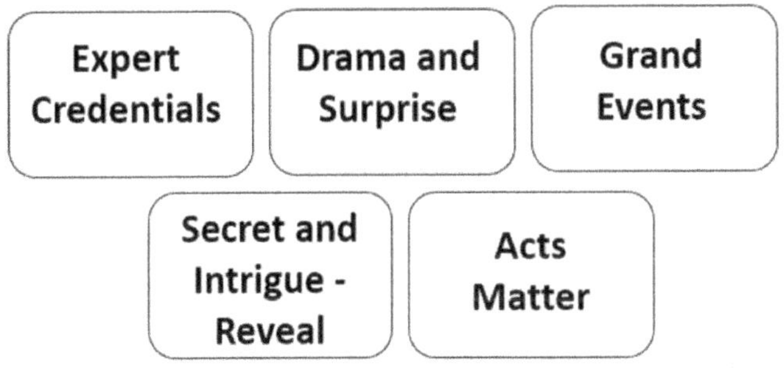

The Action Plan

An action plan for a PR-worthy event usually requires planning at least three-six months in advance. The key steps are broadly as follows:

1. Often, the first step involves the groundwork. This includes identifying the period (day or date) when the brand would like to unveil the campaign. It's usually an important day, say Valentine's Day or an Earth Day, so that it can be planned several months in advance.

2. Next, the brand team needs to figure out the acts that they should complete by the said date so that they provide sufficient fodder to the consumers to talk about their brand. This might involve a CSR initiative or a partnership with an NGO.

3. Also, once a PR Agency is roped in, they might recommend commissioning a formal research that the brand can use as data points to offer a story worthy enough to be shared with the news media.

4. Closer to the planned day, the brand team may have to call for a press conference or circulate notes to the larger media houses on the story that the brand wishes to share.

5. The brand can also plan an outreach event for social media influencers who can aid spreading the word about the brand with their large following. The brand can also create a relevant hashtag that can be propagated for consumers to have conversations in their circles.

6. Finally, to focus the conversation around a large event or a brand-led promotion can be announced to reveal the information that the brand wishes to share.

PR is often considered free, however, that is not the case. Any 'talkworthy' initiative requires months of planning and ample spends both in the run up to the event and in amplification of the event in order to be noticed. When used alongside a regular campaign, word-of-mouth marketing can lend credibility to a proposition and have a multiplier effect on the credibility of the same.

The Marketer's Checklist

- Events, PR, and word of mouth can often be quite useful in creating a buzz around the brand.
- Buzz marketing generates interest and builds loyalty among consumers by engaging them with their point of view or brand purpose.

- Brand can create opportunities for engagement when a new proposition is launched or a day is curated either to express the brand's purpose or by leveraging an existing calendar occasion.
- In such occasions, the brand tries to draw the consumer into the conversation through topics that the consumer can deeply relate to.
- The action plan for a PR-worthy event usually requires planning at least three-six months in advance.
- While PR is usually considered free, it actually requires ample spends to deliver optimal impact.

THE LOGIC OF CONSUMER PROMOTIONS

Consumer promotion is the one gift that the sales function of an organization really looks forward to from its marketing team.

As an 'area sales manager' based out of Vijayawada in 2005, I used to really look forward to the Chopper Promo, Bayblade Promo, and such similar promos, that the Bournvita brand would sport once a quarter. In that month, we would do 60% of the quarter's volumes and the sales team and the trade would really look forward to the same. So, when our organization decided to put a stop to a practice which had been a norm in the category for over a decade, I was naturally shocked. Sitting in Andhra Pradesh where we had a sub-10% market share, we found our hearts sinking.

The rationale being: one less promo every quarter, meant far more money for thematic advertising and as a salesperson then I didn't agree with the strategy at all. By the end of the year, I had to grudgingly accept that the strategy appeared to work and we gained share. But are consumer promos a necessary evil or do they have relevance in the armoury of a marketer?

Strategic Rational

There are primarily two brand tasks that a marketer must choose:

1. Grow category
2. Steal share

> Now, consumer promotions, which basically
> mean giving something free, are rarely useful
> as mediums of growing a category. Since
> you would agree to buy something extra only
> if the category is already relevant to you.
> Hence, consumer promotions usually find a
> role for a brand seeking to 'steal share' from a
> dominant market leader.

Moreover, there are several ways of running consumer promotions and it's important to decide why one would choose one route over the other.

Consumer Promotions—Broad Routes

Consumer promos are essentially routes of offering higher value to the consumer, usually for a limited period. Hence, before one recommended a consumer promo, one needs to evaluate the exact value gap that one is trying to bridge.

There are broadly three reasons for choosing to run a consumer promotion:

1. To enhance imagery
2. To bridge an imagery gap
3. To offer value

Enhancing imagery usually happens through the route of aspirational partnerships; this is often observed among alcohol brands. For instance, take the partnership between a brand of Scotch and Harley Davidson. The aspirational nature of both brands rubs off each other and creates a lucrative experience for the consumer.

The second route of bridging an imagery gap is better explained through the promo of Uncle Chips with Motu Patlu tazos. Here, the ambition is to make the brand look cool in the absence of a strong brand proposition or advertising.

The third route is the simplest where one offers a 20% extra, a Paytm cash back or free 2 GB data on a particular purchase. This route also includes promos like lucky draws offering vacations, and so on. This is usually the simplest route.

Enhancing Imagery

This is perhaps the only route of running promos that I would advocate as a sustainable strategy. A few diverse examples that come to my mind are:

1. **Luxury liquor and complimentary luggage:** At times, air travelers get complimentary exquisite luggage on the purchase of luxury liquor brands like Jonnie Walker or Chivas Regal Whiskys in duty-free shops at the airports. Here, it's critical to ensure that the craftsmanship of the gift matches the aspirational value of the brand. One of the reasons why alcohol brands invest heavily here is because you get your brand trademarks inside the house of a consumer.

2. **Bajaj Auto vs. series of bikes:** I guess Bajaj Auto saw the range of bikes 'V' that they had launched in 2016—using the 'invincible metal' from the decommissioned India's first aircraft carrier INS Vikrant—as a separate brand rather than a consumer promo. Now, it was definitely brilliant marketing and made for lovely storytelling, but the bikes quickly lost their luster and had no takers after a few years.

    This, for me, is another example of the fact that you can only borrow equity for a while and provide a halo and not buy equity permanently. The lack of their ability to sustain the range is for me another validation that the consumer perhaps only saw the range as a consumer promo rather than brand building.

3. **Coca Cola personalized labels:** If you ask me, the personalized labels launched by Coke is the king of consumer promotions. You are still just giving something 'extra' through a personalized label. But it fits well with Coke's proposition and the emotional kick it provides puts it in the category of consumer promos that enhance imagery.

4. **Britannia Khao, World Cup Jao:** This was a promo that Britannia has run a number of times since the 90s. Now, the reason why this worked is not because of the sheer value offered, but because, for a purchase of just ₹5, Britannia could fulfill your international travel aspiration. As India continues to become more affluent, the relevance of such a promo continues to wane.

The pitfall of this approach is that they rarely provide an immediate sales lift and work far more as a strategic and long-term brand building vehicle. So, if you are planning to use an Imagery Enhancing promo for next quarter's numbers, its best to think again.

Bridge an Imagery Gap

Now, this is a category of promos that I consider truly dangerous to brand equity. This is one of the easiest mistakes that marketers can make where we try and replace an equity building campaign with a promo that builds off the imagery of another brand.

Some of the examples that come to my mind as we discuss this category are as follows:

1. **Malted food drinks:** Brands like Bournvita, Horlicks, and Milo till the early 2000s used to offer a promo every quarter. We would all be truly excited about the sales lift, but there was no real increase in consumption. Our consumers would just buy these brands and store them in their cupboards for a month or two and still consume as they regularly do.

    This led to a huge cost increase for manufacturers but did not increase consumption. Also, contrary to popular belief, promos rarely lead to penetration increase and hence you don't get any new users into the category.

2. **Uncle Chips using cartoon-branded tazos:** I feel one of the reasons behind Uncle Chips falling from grace as an aspirational brand when I was growing up has been trading their own brand equity for that of a cartoon character. In my opinion, such promos may have done better for Motu Patlu's or Pokemon's fame rather than for

Uncle Chips, and these promos, I think, are best stayed away from.

3. **Disney Partnerships:** This is where it becomes fuzzy. I am all for the lovely kids' range inspired by Disney characters that many popular brands create for clothes, stationary, tiffins, etc. As long as you are clear that 'Disney' is the brand that you are selling, you are likely to sail through and create additional value for the consumer. But Disney promos, although used tactically, have seen limited success in my experience.

So, the key question to ask yourself when evaluating such a route is, are you taking a shortcut and trying to use a popular brand to sell your current product? If so, what do you think the result would be on your own brand equity in the long term?

Offering Value

These are, of course, the simplest of promos! So many of us get swayed by a 20% extra offer, especially while buying commodities like *atta* (flour), shampoo, soaps, and so on. I guess the only place where this doesn't work is in the impulse category. When you evaluate such a promo, it's important to understand the shopper behaviour for your category. Such promos are brilliant, where the trigger to drive brand switch in a category is driven by pantry stock rather than impulse. But, if you want to eat a Cadbury Silk, a 20% extra of 5 Star chocolate is unlikely to drive the switch. However, one is very likely to switch between a Britannia Good Day and a

Sunfeast Mom's Magic. It usually plays out more when these categories are closer to commodities than brands.

A few top examples for me in this category of promos are:

1. **Paytm cashback:** These have become quite popular in the past two-three years and were used by several youth brands on the basis of the coolness offered by digital payments. However, redemption rates still remain a challenge at sub 10%.

2. **Free data packs:** This is another novelty being explored in today's world of growing digital awareness. However, in my opinion, the value offered continues to be more for its freshness and novelty rather than genuine consumer value.

3. **Lucky draws:** A number of brands offer one big gift, say for e.g., a free international vacation package or a SUV to grab eyeballs, and spread the same across a large number of consumers through a lucky draw. Again, something that surely optimizes spends but only offers new news rather than sustainable growth.

4. **20% extra:** This is perhaps the most common consumer promo possible and has been extensively used in categories like tea, biscuits, etc., where the behaviour is of low involvement and habit forming. A brand with much lesser market share can nibble away at the market leader as they can run this promo with much lesser hit to their bottom line.

This puts the market leader into a catch-22 position. If you match the promo, you don't have money for brand building; if you don't, you lose share. Hence, this is an ideal weapon in the armory of a brand looking to steal share.

Consumer promos from the point of view of a pristine marketer are a necessary evil. They give you popularity with the sales team and are an easy way to drive excitement and short-term business growth. However, in the long term, they weaken your profit and loss and reduce your ability to build a branded play. Hence, these are best used tactically and infrequently to deliver the job required at the time and not as a substitute for brand building. However, before one spends money for the same, it's crucial to understand how they speak to your brand task and deliver the return on investment as expected.

The Marketer's Checklist

- Consumer promotions usually find a role for a brand seeking to 'steal share' versus a dominant market leader.
- There are broadly three reasons for choosing to run a consumer promotion:
  1. Enhance imagery
  2. Bridge an imagery gap
  3. Offer value
- The promotions that enhance imagery rarely provide an immediate sales lift and work far more as a strategic and long-term brand building vehicle.
- Brands also often collaborate with other brands with higher equity to generate rub-offs through an aspirational partnership.
- Offering value in terms of a 20% extra or a small freebee like a sticker or tazo are the simplest forms of promos.
- Promos are an easy way to drive excitement and short-

term business growth. However, in the long term, they may weaken your profit and loss, and reduce your ability to build a branded play.

USE OF CELEBRITIES IN MARKETING

As a marketer, I am always appreciative
of celebrities, because they are individuals
who have successfully reinvented
themselves as brands.

Therefore, everything that we hold true of brands, holds true for celebrities as well. They can be represented by a brand ladder much like conventional brands so they have attributes, functional and emotional identifiers.

Like we learnt about the Brand Ladder, celebrities build their fame by owning certain attributes which lead up to functional benefits and eventually imprint themselves in our mind with clear emotional cues. A few examples are as follows:

Shah Rukh Khan possesses a certain swagger, a signature pose, and a romantic hero image as his attributes. These add up to the functional benefits of enjoying an emotional family drama with all the narratives that we as Indians love. He even ladders up to a clear emotional identifier of an ideal embodiment of Indian middle-class values.

On the other hand, Akshay Kumar, with his presence on reality TV show *'Khatron Ke Khilari'* and his bold act with

Levi's jeans represents a cool action hero, his functional identifiers ladder up to a comical action figure and his emotional signature is often that of simplistic patriotism.

Therefore, it's easier to understand celebrities as brands. No wonder marketers find them very useful in seeding right values or personalities associated with their brands. I guess the best use of celebrities with brands can be bucketed into following broad areas:

1. Be noticed
2. Improve communication efficiency
3. Strengthen the brand
4. Solve a problem

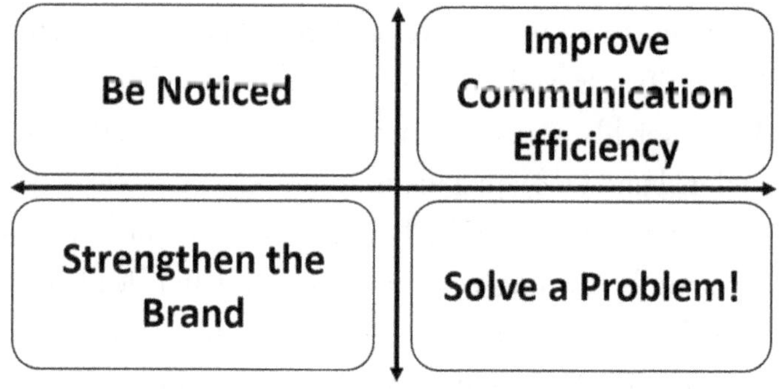

1. Be noticed

I guess this is the simplest reason for brands to leverage celebrities for their status and popularity. The advantage of such an approach is that while you may have to pay a large sum to a celebrity, you can make a splash in the market and arrive on the scene. The advantages that a brand gets in such an approach is a high talk value and buzz among consumers. This can be followed by curiosity and a number of consumers may even investigate the services that the brand offers. A few top examples of the same are:

Cred: I guess many of us are still scratching our heads over the fuss surrounding the credit card bill payment platform in a country where few people trust and use credit cards, let alone proactively bank with such companies and use credit points. How can a service like Cred effectively gain so much of attention from both investors and marketers, although I'm not too sure about the consumers who prefer using debit cards and online payments more. Whether it was the Anil Kapoor, Madhuri Dixit Nene ad series or the recent Rahul David ad, Cred definitely ensured that it got noticed!

Pan Bahar: The pan masala brand surely garnered attention when the Irish actor and film producer Pierce Brosnan, known for playing the fictional British secret agent James Bond, endorsed the product. However, the actor was particularly unhappy when he realized that he was kept in the dark about the product's harmful nature by the manufacturers. This example also demonstrates the power that PR has to provide a multiplicative effect to any celebrity-linked spends.

Levi Strauss & Co.: Of course, Levi's achieved the same impact in style when they tied up with Indian film actor Akshay Kumar in April 2009 as a part of their 'Live Unbuttoned' campaign and paid a king's ransom to Akshay. This was a time when Levi's only executed global campaigns and rarely marketed their products at country level. So, when a popular Indian film actor endorsed their product, they naturally got noticed by the youth of the country, especially after Twinkle Khanna (Indian author, interior designer, and Akshay Kumar's wife) unbuttoned his jeans at a fashion show.

2. Improve communication efficiency

I guess this is one of the most common reasons for leveraging a celebrity. When a brand has limited spends at its disposal, they fear that their communication will get lost in the media clutter or they worry that they won't be able to outshout their key competition. In this case, the use of a celebrity would ensure creative cut-through. This is the ability of a brand's communication to be noticed or recalled by its target group.

The key question that a brand manager needs to evaluate here is: Would the cost of the celebrity justify the equivalent reduction in media expenditure? Because roping in a celebrity is quite expensive and can often cost as much as 20% of the brands media budgets for the year.

Brands that work with celebrities for this purpose are:

Harpic: Now, disinfectants are not the most glamorous of the categories, and would have limited spends for their outlay. Even in such a category, Harpic is perhaps a stronger brand than others in the market and roping in Akshay Kumar would definitely be helping their case. At a daily cost of a couple of crores, you may have lesser money to spend in running your advertising but at the end of the year the impact created with consumers may justify the additional costs of the celebrity.

Balaji Wafers: Definitely not the most aspirational brand in the category, but when you have a solid promise—in terms of a much higher grammage of the product—perhaps you only need to ensure that the limited spends that you deploy on media works hard. Now, they have roped in Indian actor Ayushmann Khurrana as their brand ambassador to deliver on this task. However, given that Khurrana has a modest following as compared to Akshay Kumar, his ability to deliver on this task may be questionable.

Lux Cozi: '*Scent wali vest hain, sub se best!*' Now, that's a product tagline and advertisement that wouldn't generate interest by itself. Clearly, actor Varun Dhawan did a good job and brought some traction in a category that's likely to be of least attraction to most of us. Dhawan with his comic personality entertains, while stars like Salman Khan and Akshay Kumar endorsing other vest brands only bring in the aspect of generic masculinity.

3. Strengthen brand values

This is perhaps one of the crucial reasons why I personally advocate that brands should work with celebrities. Because it is a purely strategic marketing decision and not tactical. Celebrities represent certain values, and if you have a brand that truly belongs to the same archetype as a popular celebrity, then the mix ends up benefiting both the brand and the celebrity. Some top examples of brands that have struck gold through their celebrity associations are:

Lux: The brand has literally crafted its brand proposition on the power of celebrities as '*Filmi sitaron ki pasand*'. It, therefore, comes as no surprise when the brand collaborated with Deepika Padukone, the most successful Bollywood actress of our time.

Thums Up: The combination of Salman Khan and Thums Up remains my personal favorite. This collaboration best explains the power of finding the perfect correlation between a brand and a celebrity's personality.

Mountain Dew: This sweet, citrus-flavoured drink is an iconic and niche brand with a distinctive personality. It is no wonder that the brand rarely had to struggle in finding the right endorser. Its partnership with Indian actor and fitness entrepreneur Hrithik Roshan makes for a compelling fit.

Too Yumm!: And finally, I feel Too Yumm! did a great job of roping in Indian cricketer Virat Kohli as an ideal fit of their healthy snacking proposition.

4. Solve a problem

Sometimes collaborating with a celebrity is not just a choice, but a requirement. This strategy comes in handy when a brand faces a PR backlash and there is an urgent need to provide reassurance and re-establish trust with their consumers. Take, for instance, following examples:

Cadbury Dairy Milk Chocolates: A best example of such troubleshooting dates back to 2003-04 when Cadbury roped in veteran Indian actor Amitabh Bachchan while the confectionary giant was facing a massive credibility challenge owing to the worm infestation in their Dairy Milk chocolates. After seeing a huge loss of face with its consumers in Mumbai and business collapsing, the brand made all the right moves by signing up Amitabh Bachchan as their ambassador during the launch of its 'purity sealed' pack. The veteran actor brought back massive credibility for the brand and helped them tide over what was perhaps the largest challenge the brand had ever faced in the country.

Vicco Vajradanti: The toothpaste is possibly one of the oldest brands we are all familiar with, yet many of us may have never used it as consumers. The brand had a classic advertisement that we would see in the cinema halls in the 80s and 90s; and the brand was undoubtedly seen as jaded and belonging to the past generation. They, therefore, attempted to revive their image by collaborating with Alia Bhatt, the youth icon and popular Indian film actor, to appeal to a younger audience.

The Ground Rules

As we have gone through a number of examples, we must now understand a few ground rules that a brand must follow to ensure that the celebrities they collaborate with work as strong assets for the brand:

1. **Consistency:** To be of real value to brands, consistency is key. Whether you are an A-lister from Bollywood or an Instagram influencer, the key asset that brands look for is consistency. Hence, celebrities who represent clear core values tend to be valued more.

2. **Differentiation:** Often quirky, lesser-known celebrities can deliver great value to brands as long as they are clearly differentiated from the crowd. This helps brands stand out, thanks to those associations.

3. **Exclusivity:** Now, this goes against the grain of what a celebrity would want. A celebrity would want as many endorsements as possible not just as a source of earning but really as a way of extending his or her fame. However, what brands truly seek is a celebrity that is not already over exposed so that the connection gets clearly attributed to the brand.

Aamir Khan had endorsed Coca Cola for over a decade and when the brand decided against renewing its contract with the Indian actor in 2011, there was speculation if Khan would now endorse rival Cola brands. However, endorsing competing brands corrodes the appeal of both the brand and the celebrity as it leads to confusion in the minds of consumers and hence it's something that both brands and celebrities avoid.

Hence, collaborating with an endorser is always a crucial decision to be made carefully and with diligence. It's no doubt that right collaboration can provide huge gains for the brands and the celebrity alike, but not leveraging the celebrity well can cause wastage of moneys that could have been better deployed elsewhere.

The Marketer's Checklist

- Celebrities are individuals who have successfully reinvented themselves as brands. They, therefore, offer an opportunity for strong associations which aid brand building.
- Brands can leverage a celebrity association to deliver on the following tasks:
  1. Be noticed
  2. Improve communication efficiency
  3. Strengthen brand values
  4. Solve a problem
- Brands can work with celebrities to deliver a rapid build-up of awareness through talk value and buzz amongst consumers.
- Brands collaborate with celebrities to deliver creative cut-through or the ability of a communication to be noticed or recalled by the brand's target group.
- Celebrities represent values and if you have a brand that truly belongs to the same archetype as the popular celebrity then the mix ends up benefiting both the brand and the celebrity.
- The status and reputation of celebrities also come in handy when a brand faces a sudden PR backlash and there is an urgent need to provide reassurance and re-establish trust with their consumers.
- For celebrities to serve as assets of a brand, it's important to ensure consistency, differentiation, and exclusivity.

MAKING THE MEDIA PLAN

Once you have a strategy and budget in place, how does one go about allocating resources and building the actual execution plan? How does a marketer decide the number of resources to be invested in advertising, digital, print, radio, and new-age media? Further, there are even more complicated questions, like do I want to put my money in advertising or consumer engagement? What about digital?

The steps in making an effective media plan are often quite straightforward:
- What's my campaign objective?
- Roles of various media elements.
- Mix of advertising versus consumer engagement.
- The marketing plan - connecting the dots.

What's My Campaign Objective?

While there can often be several types of campaign objectives, the most common ones are:
- To drive 'salience'
- To drive 'consideration'
- Or 'persuasion'

Now, frankly all these objectives sound very similar, but let's understand them one at a time. A 'salience plan' is usually a 'maintenance plan'. You already have a strong brand that stands for something unique and you want to use this opportunity to keep the brand and its proposition salient in people's minds. So, the salience plans are usually the simplest ones where you chase a medium with highest reach and optimal cost and go ahead and blast your creative edits. So, if Lux or Cadbury Dairy Milk or Coca Cola wishes to remind you that they are the best existing brands during your purchasing decision, they will possibly build a salience plan.

The next type of campaign objective (to drive consideration) is where you need to push just a little harder. So, you have a brand with fairly good awareness, but it's either more expensive than competition or has benefits that are not as obvious. In such cases, just sharing your brand's message may not be good enough. That's when you start looking at additional media elements to shift consumer behaviour. For instance, brands such as Kellogg's Breakfast Cereal, Gillette Mach 3 Razor Blades, or Tropicana Juice may need to invest in this area.

Finally, the hardest-working plans are those intended to drive 'persuasion' or directly impact actual purchase. In these cases, the brand is clearly interested in ensuring a lift in the sales of the product by convincing the consumer to make a purchase. So, a Saffola World Heart Day, HDFC Life Insurance or an automobiles company may make more of these plans.

Role of Media Elements

Next, we understand the various types of media elements at your disposal and the roles that each of them play in meeting your campaign objectives.

TV/YouTube: These mediums usually have the highest reach and are hence the most impactful ones. These are usually the lead media elements in any given media plan. They offer you highest reach at lowest costs as well as engagement. As in, they are simply used to send out messages but not receive them. You passively consume the content from these media devices without actually getting any direct response from the consumers. These mediums are usually great for execution of salience plans.

Radio/Facebook/Instagram: Now, these make for an effective secondary medium and serve as a great follow-up medium. These mediums are often defined at moderate scale but receive high engagement from the audience through polls, 'call-in discussions', encouraging conversations, etc. So, if you have a complicated proposition, you can use these mediums to have an engaging discussion with your consumers. Hence, plans that 'drive consideration' usually invest here as well.

Print/Outdoor/Banner Ads on News Apps: These mediums are usually quite expensive and often used only when you have exhausted your kitty in the first two buckets. These mediums have their specific advantages; for example, print is great at providing detailed information about your product like in the case of a car or a property purchase. At the same time, outdoor advertising is great at delivering a topical message, say a range of Diwali gift offers just before Diwali.

I have elaborately used digital medium as a part of the types of elements, as it offers a versatile way of delivering the same tasks in the mainstream media with limited budgets. However, I have always found mainstream media choices to be more effective provided you have the required scale to invest in them.

Mix of Advertising vs. Consumer Engagement

> The next piece to understanding your consumer is to figure out the mix of advertising vs. consumer engagement. While both sound quite similar, at the end of the day, it is simply about a brand engaging with its consumers.

However, the real difference between 'advertising' and 'consumer engagement' is that, advertising is about sending out your brand's proposition onto the consumer, expressing the identity of your brand, and giving the consumer a unique reason to prefer your brand. Consumer engagement, on the other hand, is about figuring out what your consumer is passionate about and being able to participate in that conversation in a manner that's expected from the brand.

Now, advertising is arguably more efficient and usually the first port of call. It can also be skillfully executed by large-scale mediums like TV and YouTube. This route is also the most efficient in growing awareness and brand recall, especially for young brands.

However, the moment your campaign objective becomes complicated or if you need to engineer brand shift, the role of engagement grows. Engagement is also a great way of building brand loyalty and 'brand love'. Therefore, a brand that engages regularly has more stickiness in the minds of the consumer.

The Marketing Plan—Connecting the Dots

Let me now demonstrate how you will use the above thinking through a set of examples.

1. If you are a large brand like Lux and you want your brand to achieve 'top-of-mind' awareness in your consumers, you should regularly invest in television commercials which are able to reach a very large audience at a reasonable cost per contact.

2. At the same time, if you are a challenger brand that needs to disrupt competition, and challenge existing views of the consumer, you will possibly rely on radio or digital medium to shake existing consumer views like Pepsi did in the U.S. through their successful 'Pepsi Challenge'. They had invited consumers to take a blind taste test between Pepsi and Coke; majority of the consumers had picked Pepsi over Coke back then.

3. Again, when it comes to brands that offer complicated services like insurance, real estate, or automobiles, the consumers usually need a lot more convincing. This is

where mediums like print become effective as they are able to provide detailed information of the services.

4. For that time of the year when you need to drive a massive amount of business in a short period, topical, low-scale mediums like outdoor advertising become more relevant. This works best during occasions like Diwali when brands, especially clothing brands, communicate their offers to consumers who are seeking to buy in large numbers for gifting purposes.

5. You will remember an advertisement only if it is impactful enough. However, consumer engagement, you may have ever participated in, leaves a lasting impact. Thus, campaigns involving consumers like Saffola World Heart Day, P&G #ShareTheLoad, and Gillette Mach 3: Women Against Lazy Stubble can leave a long-lasting impact that often spurs brand love and loyalty.

Media teams in any organization play a crucial role in helping the brand team make and execute exciting marketing plans. However, the process is always collaborative and starts with complete clarity on the brand and campaign objectives. These initiatives usually have clear metrics that are studied for business impact and shifts in consumer behaviour. However, it's crucial for marketers to build sustainable long-term strategies that can be executed consistently for a lasting impact.

The Marketer's Checklist

*   In order to make an ideal media plan, it's important to start from the campaign objective, devise the role of

various media objectives, arrive at the optimal mix of advertising and consumer engagement before making the final marketing plan.

- A media plan usually has one of the three key objectives — salience, consideration, or persuasion.
- Media elements such as TV, radio, print, outdoor advertising, etc., are plotted against the objectives that they are best suited to deliver upon.
- Next, we evaluate the mix of advertising and consumer engagement.
- Advertising is about sending out your brand's proposition onto the consumer, expressing the identity of your brand, and giving the consumer a unique reason to prefer your brand.
- Consumer engagement, on the other hand, is about participating in the passion points of your consumers in the brand's unique voice.
- A brand campaign eventually delivers on the business objectives by achieving its identified campaign objectives.

4

BUILDING THE MIX

Building a Winning Product
Role of Pricing in Business Decision Making
How to Evaluate Packaging Design
How to Deliver Innovations That Work
Building the Right Brand Architecture

BUILDING A WINNING PRODUCT

I have worked across several product categories — chocolates, biscuits, alcohol, and cheese. However, it has always been a challenge to understand how one decides which product is better than the other. Is Cadbury Dairy Milk Chocolate bar better than Nestlé Classic Milk Chocolate Bar or is Britannia Good Day a better biscuit than Sunfeast Mom's Magic? Of course, alcohol is a fascinating category with Chivas Regal and Johnnie Walker being fine scotch whisky brands, but which one is better of the two?

Hence, I realized that while the product is core to the business that we are in, it's not easy to articulate what differentiates our product from our competitive brands, especially in a consumer-facing manner.

We know that Britannia Cheese is yellow-orange in colour than Amul Cheese, which is whitish. But does the colour of the cheese here really matters to the consumer or is it the saltiness of the cheese? How does the consumer make a decision on what product they'd enjoy more, or what attributes do they really notice?

Often, we rely on crutches like the recipe, a trademarked formula, or nutritional benefits. Although a consumer can read these details on a label, the thing that actually builds loyalty and drives repeats is the consumer's actual experience of using a product.

A consumer may know that a biscuit has better health claims than another, but often these details may not represent a compelling difference or align with what the consumer truly values when making that brand choice.

Often, a consumer might state that they love a product and are a loyal user. However, when questioned how it's different from its competition, they might struggle to explain the reasons and may not even recognize the product in question during a blind tasting.

So, how do marketers go about understanding this consumer psyche and consequently strengthen their offers? Let's find the answer in this section.

The Product Experience

> When asked to describe the product
> experience as a consumer, we often use
> words that marketers have taught us.
> While describing the experience of drinking
> a whisky, we say it's "smooth", a soap
> feels "silky", and a bar of chocolate is
> "drool-worthy".

But isn't it baffling to compare the smoothness of one whisky with another or the silkiness of the lather of one soap with another?

Hence, the first step for any marketer is to arrive at a list of attributes which consumers can compare and rate. These could include a number of sensory attributes like:

- Physical attributes: colour, viscosity, density, and visuals.
- Organoleptic attributes: taste, aroma, and feeling.
- Physiological impact: satisfaction on swallowing, feeling of fullness, feeling of softness on hands post using the product, etc.

Once we arrive at the attributes which can be discerned by a sufficiently sophisticated observation and compared, we now have the right attributes to study consumer preference.

Product Evaluation

The products can then be evaluated in two ways—either through a panel of experts or directly by consumers. The experts are typically trained to possess a keen awareness of the product experience and the difference between products. Often such experts are 'master blenders' as used in alco-bev or in the tea industry. However, testing with consumers is more relevant when it comes to its real world application.

> Testing with consumers is often done through a formal testing technique known as a 'product test' where the sample and the 'control' are tested with a statistically significant number of consumers.

The 'control' typically represents a 'gold standard' against which the sample is expected to win in order to meet the protocols for launch. A significant number of consumers is decided upon by the degree of accuracy or results expected by the researchers linked to the criticality of the decision for the business.

Product Testing

Product testing in consumer goods organizations is usually done for two reasons—renovation and innovation.

- Renovation is often done when the existing product is changed. The need for change may arrive because an improved recipe is available. It's often done due to cost pressures where there is a need to reduce recipe cost without compromising upon the consumer experience. In such a case, the product testing is done against the existing product and often a more stringent significance level is sought. One of the biggest pitfalls of cost optimization across the years is that after two or three renovations, the new product may be much poorer in experience than the original product. And hence R&D teams are encouraged to maintain the original recipe as the 'gold standard' to understand how the consumer experience is changing over the years.

- Innovation is often done when a new product is introduced and there is no internal 'gold standard' available. In such cases, the product testing is done against a competitive product. This competitive product could be a direct competition or a 'source of business'. Say we are launching a new 100% juice brand. In such a case, Tropicana 100% could be a direct competition while a regular Tropicana could be a 'source of business'. In categories that are niche, the 'source of business' might be a better benchmark and then a 'significant superiority' is sought.

In both cases, the methodology of arriving at a superior product remains the same, only the benchmark product to be tested against and the degree of superiority sought changes against an agreed set of attributes.

Testing Protocols

In order to ensure an unbiased testing, researchers need to make sure that a set of guidelines is laid out to maintain consistency. A few points to consider across industries are as follows:

- **Avoiding branding bias:** Often a lot of consumer bias creeps in if the consumers are aware of the brand they are testing. Precisely for this reason, the consumers are often blindfolded and asked to give genuine responses.
- **Usage experience:** The usage experience of products differs. Testing for detergents, food, or cosmetics would differ. In each category, the product testing protocol must cater to the kind of usage the product sees to get relevant outcomes.
- **Food testing:** Even within food categories, products might be consumed directly, used as taste enhancers or as an ingredient. The testing protocol must take into account the actual point of usage to arrive at the most important part of the consumption journey for testing.

The most important part of the mix is often the product. However, in order to arrive at a fair evaluation of our product against the competition, we must first arrive at a logical set of product attributes which we can enhance or modify to garner appeal with the consumers. Once these attributes are arrived at, they must be tested against competition to arrive at our right to win, whether we are planning an innovation or a renovation. These testing protocols must assess the product at the point of usage that truly matters to the consumer to help us arrive at an optimal understanding of our offer.

The Marketer's Checklist

- In the creation of a good product, it's important for the marketer to go beyond obvious factors such as nutritional value and ingredients, and consider things that the consumer truly values.
- Hence, the marketer must arrive at a list of attributes which consumers can compare and rate like physical attributes, organoleptic attributes, physiological attributes among others.
- Testing with consumers is often done through a formal testing technique known as a 'product test' where the sample and the 'control' are tested with a statistically significant number of consumers.
- The 'control' is usually a 'gold standard' against which the sample is expected to win to pass the protocols for launch.
- Product testing in consumer goods organizations is usually done for two reasons—renovation and innovation.
- Product development in—the case of renovation—is typically about improving taste parameters which the consumer values while optimizing recipe cost.

- On the other hand, in the case of innovation, product development is usually about beating the competition or source of business on product parameters which the consumer values.

ROLE OF PRICING IN BUSINESS DECISION-MAKING

Pricing is perhaps the decision that has the most direct correlation to business' bottom line. Hence, the profit profile that you wish to hold depends upon the pricing decisions that you are willing to take. If you price the product too high, then the competition may undercut you. If you price it too low, you will not have the margins required for investment. So, how do marketing professionals go about making this crucial decision?

While there are several subtle nuances, let me start with the business basics on the key pricing positions that any player in the market can decide to explore.

Pricing Landscape

There are four intuitive positions that most companies may consider when they review their portfolio:
1. Mass
2. Premium
3. Super Premium
4. Affordable

Now, given that the majority of my experience has been in India, the most common price position that is considered here is at 'mass tier'. Products like Good Day biscuits, Blenders Pride whisky, Kit Kat chocolate are best-suited examples of brands that operate at healthy profits and offer their services to the vast majority of the great Indian middle class.

The next tier is 'premium'. In my experience, a price band of 1.2x to 1.3x of the mass tier is crucial to build a relevant business at a premium position. Now, this premium of 20-30% is crucial as my empirical learnings suggest that the consumer is comparatively flexible within this price band. The consumer is usually willing to upgrade if they are given enough reasons to do so.

The 'super-premium band' is a wide band that exists from anywhere above 1.3x to 10x of the mass tier. However, it requires providing a significantly distinct experience. Few brands, products, and companies are able to offer the experience required to charge that premium.

The final tier that I will talk about is the 'affordable tier'. This is when a product or business is able to offer an experience quite close to the benchmark at the mass tier at a pricing that is 0.7- 0.8 x of the mass tier. This typically requires quite a stretch, as it often becomes a volume game at wafer-thin margins.

Rationale for Mass Pricing

Most of us just look at market benchmarks while deciding pricing, however, what is the actual rational logic that determines this crucial decision?

> Pricing rationale eventually comes down to profits. Most corporates would like to deliver a bottom line that is at least 2x of bank interest. Hence, the corporate sector aims to earn a net operating income of 12 to 15% of the Net Sales Value (NSV).

The cost of goods, advertising spends, and business overheads that can be sustained while delivering 12-15% operating income is what leads to the pricing for a mass player.

The mass pricing strategy is, of course, extremely vulnerable to attacks from the top and bottom pricing positions. So, it requires stringent quality checks, product consistency, and consistent brand building to fend off attacks. Examples of companies that have done this well include Cadbury Dairy Milk (which has been the gold standard of chocolates for the longest time), Good Day in biscuits, Surf in detergents, and Lux in soaps.

The Premium Position

Usually, the most attractive position in any market is the premium position, as it enables an organization to participate in a reasonable business size with subtle differentiation. Also, given a similar cost of goods, a premium position can garner as much as 4x of profits of the mass player at 50% of the scale. Some of the examples of products that have managed to justify and hold a premium position in the market include Cadbury Dairy Milk Silk in chocolates and Dove in soaps.

This price position usually requires substantial product differentiation as well as aggressive investment in brand building. The visible marker of product differentiation in Cadbury Dairy Milk Silk is its position of the softest, meltiest chocolate, and that of Dove—a soap with 1/4th moisturizing cream.

Further, a rationale needs to be built in your mind to spend more. You buy Cadbury Silk for that intimate, indulgent moment where only the best chocolate will do. Similarly, you buy Dove to preserve your real, natural beauty through hydrated skin. Product differentiation as well as the rationale to spend that 30% extra needs to ring in your mind each time you buy the product.

The Super Premium Strategy

The strategy that I have seen most often fail is the super premium strategy, especially in the Indian context. This is because we, as consumers, are skeptical and well-informed, and pride ourselves on buying smart. The moment a product breaches the 1.3x pricing position, we instantly become skeptical. A few brands that have been unable to garner scale in the Indian landscape at such a position are Bournville chocolates, Good Day chunkies, and the premium scotch category in the country.

Bournville invested in some brilliant advertising, touting its claims of being made from pure Ghanaian cocoa and presenting an exciting proposition of 'You Have to Earn It'. But believe me, carrying off such a premium position even with the best product in the Indian landscape requires a fundamentally superior degree of brand building.

Another category that comes to mind is that of whisky.

When a consumer consumes an Imperial Blue, Royal Challenge, or a Blenders Pride, the richness of taste often can help pull apart differences. However, it is often difficult to understand why a scotch whisky like Chivas Regal would be 5 to 10 times the price of a regular whisky brand like Imperial Blue or Royal Challenge.

A brand that I believe has managed to successfully carry off a super-premium priced position is Epigamia Greek yogurt—against other flavoured yogurts with a clear demonstrable claim of superiority of offering double the protein as normally offered by regular-flavoured yogurts.

The crucial learning here is that consumers are often willing to pay 20-30% higher to move to a better product. For example, a consumer of Parle-G may happily spend a little more to consume Good Day because of the promise of butter or dry fruits. However, when the consumer is expected to pay between 50 and 100% more than their current choice, then they need a whole new reason to buy a particular product; say for instance, the consumer would be willing to pay for biscuits in a tin box for gifting purpose even if it's sold at a much higher price.

Affordable Game Plan

The final pricing strategy that I would like to cover is the one which involves guerrilla warfare. Believe me, when going against an established player, it's not easy to pull off an affordable price position of 75-80% of the mass player. A few brands that have managed to do this well are CavinKare's CHIK Shampoo (with their 50 paisa shampoo sachets) and

Parle-G biscuits. There have also been a few disasters here, including the famous Tata Nano car.

Now, CHIK shampoo carried this off by delivering at a massive scale. The legend has it that when Unilever realized the behemoth that CHIK shampoo had become, they were offering more shampoo in terms of volume just through the 50 paisa shampoo sachets than all of Unilever's shampoos put together. It's the same with Parle-G. Most companies believe that the cost of the raw material would be higher than the cost of the biscuit packets. Then how do such companies manage to pull off these insanely low prices?

The game plan again goes back to the profit and loss statement. If you are not compromising on the cost of goods or advertising spends, the only cost head that you can leverage is company overheads. What this means is that most mass players rely on a logical cost of operations, be it sales and distribution, employee costs, and bonuses. You need to operate with extremely low employee costs to justify such a price position.

Next, having depreciated assets like old and large factories also helps as long as flexibility in operation is not required. However, this makes these brands extremely vulnerable to consumer evolution.

Tata Nano was launched with much fanfare and was expected to provide an affordable option to millions of two-wheeler users across the country. However, instead of being seen as an affordable upgrade from two-wheelers, consumers saw it as a 'cheap' car that was no longer aspirational. Hence, it failed to garner any traction across the country.

To sum it up, there are several price positions that brands

can take in the market. However, this decision is to be taken judiciously keeping a close eye on the total mix. A premium position requires clear markers of aspiration and demands communication. A super premium position can often become niche unless the consumer triggers are exploited smartly. An affordable position is not always a mantra to win unless the business model is well thought through. However, pricing will always remain one of the most crucial decisions a business would take, given the direct implication on the bottom line.

The Marketer's Checklist

- There are broadly four price positions that a brand can be positioned on. These are 'mass', 'premium', 'super premium', and 'affordable'.
- Mass pricing typically helps a business earn a profit margin double of the bank interest and, hence, is often in line with standard category benchmarks.
- Premium pricing is usually 20% more than mass pricing and can help maximize profit while compromising on scale.
- The super premium category exists at a pricing in excess of 30% of mass and often needs distinct codes to call out the rationale for a premium.
- Finally, affordable pricing undercuts the market leader and often needs a different formulation or technology advantage to sustain the business at high volumes but limited margins.

HOW TO EVALUATE PACKAGING DESIGN

The one part of marketing everyone believes that they are an expert of is, packaging design. Many a brand managers have nightmares getting the entire organization to align with the idea of a winning design. Could this be because design is just art and only needs a reasonable aesthetic sense? I really don't think so. In fact, my belief is quite the opposite. I believe packaging design is actually all science. While creativity brings in flair, it's essential to understand the principles that deliver a visual delight and expected business delivery.

The Science of Pack Design

Through my experiences, I have learned that pack designs are only a collection of assets. Every piece of art can be broken apart into discrete elements and one can mount a study that helps you identify how important each of these assets are.

If we study the pack designs of popular brands:

- **A bar of Lux soap:** The way Lux is written in gold, pink background colour, rose buds, words such as 'floral beauty oil', 'soft touch', 'for soft fragrant skin'.
- **A bar of 5 Star chocolate:** The gold background, Cadbury in a purple splash, icon of five stars below the name, the cut chocolate profile with caramel oozing out.
- **A pack of Good Day butter biscuits:** The blue colour of the background, the Britannia logo, 'Good Day' logo with the 'smile', butter cookies product descriptor, and splashes of butter around the cookies are all key brand assets which can be deconstructed and studied.

Next, the research can help you rate each
of these attributes on two very simple
parameters—which of these are meaningful
and which are distinctive.

Meaningful attributes are the ones that add more weight to the brand proposition or personality. Like one might say that the way Lux is written in gold is extremely meaningful as it connotes luxury and glamour. Similarly, the shots of the flowers are extremely meaningful as they connote a feeling of silky lather, or bring alive a pool full of petals.

Distinctively, it is about how unique each of these elements are. Lux is unlikely to be the only soap bar to have a pack design with flowers and, hence, flowers may not be distinctive. Again, a lot of the text might feel generic. Benefits like 'noticeable soft skin' may again be expected on a Dove soap bar. These can also be called as 'distinctive assets'.

The term 'distinctive brand assets' was coined by Jenni Romaniuk, an author and researcher at the Ehrenberg-Bass Institute. According to her, these assets act as triggers that prompt consumers to think of a particular brand name without explicitly stating it. Romaniuk, however, has a different take on this concept where she emphasizes on these assets being famous and unique.

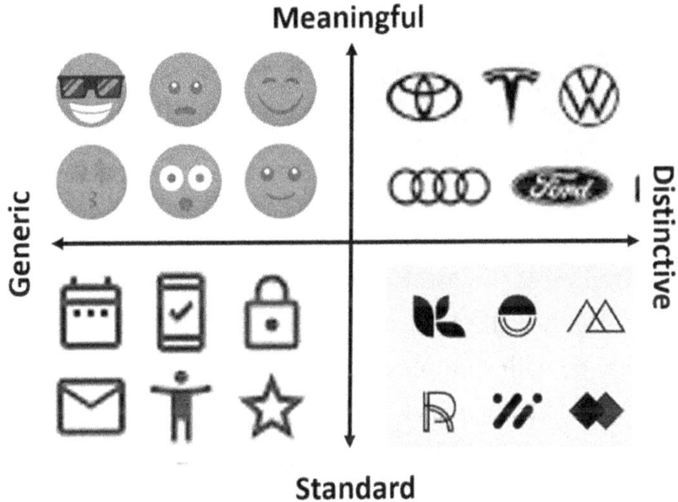

Let's take the example of 5 Star chocolate; the gold colour is extremely distinctive as it's the only chocolate brand that sports the bright gold colour. Furthermore, the cut chocolate profile with caramel oozing out is meaningful, as the most enjoyable part of 5 Star is the experience of chewy caramel consumption.

In the case of Good Day butter cookies, its logo with a smile is both distinctive as well as meaningful as it expresses its 'smiles proposition', while the colour blue for butter is meaningful but not distinctive as other butter cookies use the same colour.

Therefore, the first task for any brand manager while planning to refresh the pack design is to carry out a clear audit of their brand's pack assets and rate them on being meaningful and distinctive.

The Design Brief

Once you have audited your pack design and arrived at the rating of your assets, it's important for you to start thinking about what you want the design team to do with those assets.

So, there are several things that can be done with your pack assets:

1. Weed out the assets that are neither meaningful nor distinctive. If you see the journey of Dairy Milk, they started with a number of meaningless assets. Over time, they made their pack simpler by getting rid of everything that was not adding meaning. The big change from 1999 to 2013 was just getting rid of the white band.

2. Accentuate the assets that are both meaningful and distinctive. The most fascinating example of a brand that has done this well is Kellogg's Special K. They realized that their most meaningful and distinctive asset was 'K', so they simply blew it up on the front of the packet and came up with a design that can be spotted from a mile away.

3. Add meaning to assets that are distinctive but not necessarily meaningful. In the case of Toblerone, they have a fine triangular-shaped pack which is definitely

distinctive. But what is the meaning that it connotes? Very smartly, the makers of the brand have linked it to the triangular shape of the Matterhorn—the Swiss mountain with a distinct symmetrical shape. The design, therefore, lends further credibility to the Swiss heritage of the famous chocolate brand.

4. Take an asset that is already meaningful and make it more distinctive. For example, Oreo realized that the two assets that are most meaningful about its pack is the blue colour and the biscuit shell. In subsequent refreshes, they owned a particular shade of blue and magnified the biscuit on the pack.

5. And finally, add new assets. This is often the riskiest proposition and must be done carefully, because when you reduce the assets on the pack and make it less cluttered, you get spotted more easily on a shelf and your brand personality shines stronger. However, the moment you add new assets, you tend to alienate your core users or confuse them. Hence, one has to be extremely careful about adding anything new unless it has some substantial meaning and can accentuate the proposition. An example is the new biscuit design of Sunfeast's Mom's Magic where they added a heart symbol on the biscuit and highlighted it on the pack as well. Now, the design is not completely new, as the pack has always held a heart symbol in some shape and form. However, it's clearly an asset in which Mom's Magic is looking to hugely invest in. This way, the heart symbol —something that could have been easily missed—now appears at the core of the brand.

Packaging Design as an Element of Strategy

> Packaging design is a strong element of strategy. Understanding category and consumer codes can really help optimize investments and deliver value to the consumers.

A few examples of innovative packaging designs that have done well in recent years are:

a) **Johnnie Walker:** They use bottle weight and height to connote premiumness thereby subtly using design to charge a premium as one moves to more premium variants. In the case of Johnnie Walker Black Label, they use a black cover to emphasize the smokiness of the blend.

b) **Cadbury Dark Milk:** The pack of this new chocolate bar depicts a reverse letter 'C' (of Cadbury) as a 'D' in the 'Darkmilk' to leverage existing memory structures that have been built through the years to simply drive connections to the original Cadbury Dairy Milk thereby aiding a rapid growth of awareness and understanding.

c) **Oreo:** The brand has successfully built strong memory structures in the minds of the consumers with colour blue and unique cookies so much so that they launched their special edition Rainbow pack without any branding or fear of losing the memorability of the brand. Coca Cola uses the same understanding and technique in their various activations with personalized labels as well.

Therefore, I believe that packaging design is more of a science than art. It's about clearly identifying the assets that you own, assessing how meaningful and distinctive they are, and deciding if you are going to add meaning to distinctive assets or make meaningful assets more distinctive. The more you declutter your pack, the more iconic it becomes. Often, to strengthen or shift your proposition, new assets need to be added. However, they are best done when they are borrowed from some memory structures that are already available on your packs. This understanding also plays a meaningful role while launching new variants, premiumization, and activation. Also, a clear understanding of this theory is crucial in helping you create a great design brief and evaluate the designs suggested by your agency.

The Marketer's Checklist

- All pack designs are only a collection of assets. Every piece of art can be broken apart into discrete elements which can then be enhanced or removed.
- We then study these attributes to understand how meaningful or distinctive each of the discrete elements are.
- Meaningful attributes are those that add value to the brand proposition or personality, whereas distinctive attributes talk about how unique each of these elements are.
- Elements that are both meaningful and distinctive are very important as they serve as key branding elements and can often be enhanced.

- We can then decide whether to make meaningful assets more distinctive or to add meaning to distinctive assets.
- Elements that are neither meaningful nor distinctive can often be dropped to make key elements prominently stand out.

HOW TO DELIVER INNOVATIONS
THAT WORK

Innovation is truly the holy grail of marketing. It often feels like business growth at no cost or investment. After all, what does one really have to do when it comes to innovation? While selling more of an existing brand feels tough, launching a new innovation often feels like an easy growth opportunity. Innovation, however, is also perhaps the most precarious marketing tool. Too many brands and companies have lost their way on the back of an innovation strategy that ran wild—where you shell out too much of your money to support the new kids on the block instead of investing in your core. However, there can really never be anything more gratifying for a business when an innovation strategy succeeds.

There are several aspects surrounding innovation that are important to understand, as well as a few learnings that can guide your journey. Some of the aspects we will cover are:

- Finding big ideas
- Types of innovation
- Innovations that work and some that don't

Finding Big Ideas

> The cardinal truth of innovation is to search
> for that unmet consumer need. Remember
> what Henry Ford said, "If I had asked people
> what they wanted, they would have said
> faster horses."

Therefore, asking the consumer what they want you to launch is definitely not a great idea! So, what does one do? Where do those breakthrough ideas come from?

Most new ideas come from 'occasions'. Whatever your category may be, think of an occasion, visualize your consumer and what they do during that occasion. Can you think of a simple way to make that task easier? One of the best examples of such an innovation strategy is the launch of Crown Royal Regal Apple Flavored Whisky. Marketers noted that, in Canada, a whisky cocktail with apple juice was gaining popularity, so they launched a whisky liquor with apple flavour!

Another interesting example is that of Baileys Irish Cream Liqueur. The occasion that its maker Diageo India was trying to crack was the one where women are comfortable drinking some alcohol. Lo and behold! They created dessert occasions, especially during Christmas, that led to the launch of one of their six global giants. However, the essence is always to dive deep into the occasion and identify what you will replace as the starting point for most innovations.

Types of Innovations

Now, there are several ways of categorizing innovations. However, the framework that I find most consumer-driven is—'new news', 'new occasions', and 'new behaviours'.

New News Innovations: They are basically those innovations that replace an existing occasion. So, if you launch a new flavour or a variant, say a dark chocolate-flavoured milkshake, you are most likely to replace one of your existing milkshake occasions by this one. Recruit innovations bring in some fresh excitement to your brand, but they typically cannibalize an existing occasion and only bring in limited incremental business. Hence, it's often recommended that 'recruit innovations' should come in and replace an existing SKU to manage business efficiencies and avoid that long tail.

New Occasions Innovations: These give your existing consumer 'new reasons' to consume your brand. So, if your brand is Cadbury Dairy Milk, launching Cadbury Dairy Milk Shots offers the consumer one new occasion to consume Cadbury Dairy Milk in, say an occasion where they might previously have consumed a sugar-boiled candy. I find 're-recruit innovations' often the most successful as they need limited investment to support and yet bring reasonable incremental business.

New Behaviour Innovations: They are the most exciting and the riskiest of the innovations. Most marketers should really tread carefully here, you may be venturing into the unknown; into a territory where your existing business has limited equity. So, in my mind, the most important rule to follow with 'disruptive innovations' is to research them adequately and build a war chest that you can afford. Phase them out, perhaps no more than one or two in a year with adequate money to support them and enough research or in-market testing that the organization is ready to truly support them. An example of a disruptive innovation in recent years would be the launch of Smart TVs by Xiaomi Mi or the iWatch series by Apple.

Innovations That Work

I have had the good fortune of witnessing many successful and a few not-so-successful innovations in my career. I can broadly divide them into two clear buckets: those that worked and those that didn't. And there were some fairly intuitive rules that made the difference.

Innovations That Worked: Most of the successful innovations that I have seen, aligned to one simple golden rule—they took the brand proposition forward and avoided becoming the competition. Some examples are:

- **Cadbury Silk Oreo:** New news innovation that gives the consumer a reason to try a different Cadbury Silk and offers fresh excitement.
- **Cadbury Shots:** New occasions innovation that helps chocolates enter the candy occasions.
- **Cadbury Celebrations:** A new behaviour innovation, that turned chocolates into a modern *meetha* and an actual *mithai* replacement.

Innovations I Am Not a Fan Of: Those innovations that are too close to a competition offer are innovations that I am not a fan of. For instance:

- **Cadbury Dairy Milk Crispello:** Now, it's a recent launch and the verdict isn't out yet. But if you ask me, if I want to eat a Kit Kat, I will eat a Kit Kat! It appears to be a 'new occasion' innovation from the family of Cadbury where Perk may be chosen for a regular wafer experience while Crispello may be chosen in a more special occasion where you also wish to consume a wafery chocolate.
- **Cadbury Fuse:** Clearly this chocolate bar was launched to help Cadbury enter a new occasion of 'hunger' satiation that Snicker owns. However, the challenge being that Snickers owns the occasion too distinctively.

The Marketer's Checklist

- Ensure that your innovation ideas start from the perspective of 'consumer' or the 'occasion', rather than as a straight product idea, so you know that you are solving a genuine gap in the market.
- Build a healthy mix of all three types of innovations. 'New News Innovations' are similar to activations and keep your brand fresh. 'New Occasions Innovations' usually are the most successful. 'New Behaviour Innovations' need investment and better timing.
- Finally, innovations that work, start from the core of the brand and extend the brand's usage into new occasions or behaviours. Innovations that don't work, usually try and take on the competition in the competitor's turf!

All in all, it's a journey full of excitement and perils to be navigated thoughtfully.

BUILDING THE RIGHT BRAND ARCHITECTURE

I am sure if there is one question that has puzzled most entrepreneurs and marketers, it has to be: How many brands they need and what is the architecture that is needed to pull them together?

The reason why this question is so critical is because branding offers an identity to your products and elevates them from mere commodities. Trousers made of blue denim fabric were available before Levi's came along and bought the intellectual rights as the 'original riveted jeans' and that offered them a unique value to the consumer that is relevant even today. Thus, the identity that you create for your offerings may be the most important decision you make and have the highest link to your long-term success.

> Having the right branding architecture is critical as brands allow you to charge a premium. However, brands also need investment to remain healthy. Having too few brands may not give you the desired flexibility that you need to expand. On the other hand, you may not have the money to maintain too many brands.

The interlinkages between your brands is called a branding architecture. The way this is crafted can help you hold together all the products that you may wish to offer to your consumers.

Types of Branding Architectures

The concept of brand architecture has been written about extensively by Jean-Noël Kapferer in his book *The New Strategic Brand Management: Creating and Sustaining Brand Equity Long Term* and David Aaker in his book *Managing Brand Equity*. There are essentially four main types of branding architectures:

1. **Master brand:** This is the most intuitive architecture where the key focus of investment of an organization is on a single mega brand that defines the category your business is in. Popular examples are FedEx and Google. Google demonstrates its competence in high-tech products and offers it through various extensions like Google Search, Google Maps, Google Play, and Google Pay.

2. **Sub-brand:** As business matures and you start adding a portfolio of offerings, there is a need to offer a differentiated identity within your bouquet of offerings. That's when the sub-brand architecture becomes relevant. The various offerings from Cadbury Dairy Milk like Cadbury Dairy Milk Silk, Cadbury Dairy Milk Shots, and Cadbury Dairy Milk Crispello are all examples of sub-brands within Cadbury Dairy Milk.

3. **Endorsed brands:** There are times when there is a need

to pull apart new offerings from the mother brand and that's where endorsed brands take root. Best example here would be that of Cadbury Bournville where the promise, packaging delivery, and product itself are very distinct from the mother brand Cadbury Dairy Milk.

4. **House of brands:** This is the ultimate stage of evolution for a business where the scale and width of products that you offer to the consumer can be in varied businesses, that they have little in common with each other and the consumer may not even identify them with the master brand, say in the case of Procter & Gamble.

What's the Right Brand Architecture for Me?

So, as an entrepreneur, how should you go about choosing your branding solution? I guess the answer lies in a few crucial questions:

1. **Scale:** What is the scale that you are planning for your business in the next few years and what is your ability to invest? In case your ambitions are modest, it's best to try and work with a frugal 'master branding' architecture.

2. **Range:** What are the categories that you plan to enter? If you are planning to restrict your play to a limited set of categories, then building a master brand strategy would be easy to execute. However, if you are planning to enter a range of categories, the task becomes a lot more complex.

3. **Proposition:** Finally, the most complex question in your branding task is to identify your unique point of difference. Once you are able to identify this, you will

realize that you can build preference across a range of offers by rooting your brand in a singular emotional truth.

What Business Goals Am I Solving?

The first part of your question is to arrive at the ideal portfolio that you are building the brand architecture for. This would be achieved as follows:

1. **Category selection:** The first step is to study all the possible categories that you may be interested in entering. Next would be to understand how attractive these categories are by building an estimate on their future growth rates and profitability. This is done by observing the growth rates in the past few years and the pricing of the offerings.

2. **Market share ambition:** Once you have identified the most profitable and the fastest-growing categories, you need to build your market share ambition in these sectors based on your right to win in terms of product knowledge, sourcing efficiencies, uniqueness of your offer, etc.

3. **Business projection:** The combination of category selection and market share ambition would help you arrive at your business projections and then will emerge what brand architecture you require to solve to meet your business ambitions.

Once you have your steady range of products and the categories that you need to enter, it's time to uncover the brands you need to create and the brand stretch that you can afford.

How Do I Solve It?

This is the section where the skill of a marketer truly comes in the forefront. Here, one leverages the competition and consumer understanding to build a structure of the market. The next few phases are as follows:

1. **Competition analysis:** One needs to list out all the competing brands that we are benchmarking ourselves against. This also helps us understand how many competitive brands have been used to target consumers.

2. **Need states:** This is usually followed up with a workshop where competing brands are grouped into similar need states. For example, Oreo, Treat, Dark Fantasy can all be clubbed under a head of 'indulgence', McVitie's, NutriChoice, Nutricrunch come under 'health' category. While 50-50, KrackJack, Monaco come under 'snacking', and so on.

3. **Sizing of the need states:** Next, these 'need states' are clubbed based on the size of your ambition for these segments. If you have a large ambition for both health and snacking, you might need two brands. However, if you have modest ambitions for health, both health and crackers can be clubbed and delivered by a single brand.

4. **Associations:** Once you have arrived at the number of brands that you require. You need to now take the creative leap and arrive at the associations that you wish to link to your brand. The more emotional the associations, the

larger your ability to stretch your brand, and the more money you will need to spend to communicate your associations.

Architecture Requirements	What Goals Am I Solving?	How Do I Solve It?
Scale	Category Selection	Competition Analysis
Range	Market Share Ambition	Sizing of Need States
Proposition	Business Projection	Creation of Associations

This process is a short overview of the work that the marketing team or a competent brand consultant would take you through. Let me now demonstrate the magic that could emerge with a few compelling examples:

The winning branding solution usually creates a good link between your portfolio's points of differentiation and then takes the creative leap for an emotional benefit. It's the emotional story that primarily determines how compelling the consumer finds your brand and the stretch that the consumer allows you to take.

1. **Paper Boat:** I guess most of us would consider Paper Boat as one of our favourite brands. Hector Beverages Pvt. Ltd., first created a fabulous product—Paper Boat Aaamras—a mango juice in a unique packaging with fruit content significantly higher than its competing brands. But they didn't stop there; they then took a

step back and built their brand around a nostalgic story of 'drinks and memories'. These associations allowed the brand to stretch beyond just juices to milk-based beverages like *thandai*, a launch of a *chikki, aam papad* bar, and also traditional snacks like *bhakarwadi*.

When they introduced a sub-brand Paper Boat Swing, they wished to unlock a certain scale with a cheaper juice drink that has low fruit content.

2. **ITC Wonders:** One example of a brand that has perhaps not delivered to the expectations so far is a range of milk drinks by ITC—Sunfeast Wonderz Milk. Frankly, I love the product. It's a set of milkshakes (with promises of real fruit pulp and fruit bits) and NutShakes (flavoured with Kesar Badam and containing real *badam* (almond) bits).

    In my opinion, the challenge Wonderz faces is the lack of right associations. The brand has not been tied to a compelling product promise. However, I am quite excited to see how the new re-branding will impact the business. They have leveraged the power of Sunfeast and Dark Fantasy—their existing biscuit brands—to drive indulgence cues. This is quite efficient as you can drive more business with less brands. The emotional relevance of the Sunfeast brand may be more relevant than what they may be able to create with Wonderz.

Building the right branding architecture would perhaps be the most important decision that you would ever take. Hence, it's not a decision to be taken in haste. It's critical for you to first land your business ambitions and then lean on the right marketing support. This will help craft the most optimal architecture that is tied to the right emotional associations to enable you to meet your ambitions.

The Marketer's Checklist

- There are essentially four main types of branding architectures — master brand, sub-brand, endorsed brand, and house of brands.
- In the case of a master brand-led architecture, the focus of the organization is on a single mega brand that defines the category your business is in.
- In the case of architecture led by sub-brand, you have a portfolio of offerings each of which need to be differentiated from each other.
- In an endorsed brand architecture, there is a need to pull apart your offerings from the mother brand.
- In a house of brands architecture, the scale and width of your offerings may have little in common from each other and require distinct identities.
- The right architecture for your business depends upon the scale of the business you are attempting to build, the range of categories you wish to enter, and the proposition that ties your business together.
- In order to land at the ideal brand architecture, you must visualize your category selection, market share ambition, and build a business projection.
- The final solution entails competition analysis, identification and sizing of needs states, and building the associations which will link your portfolio to the brands you require.

5

TYPES OF MARKETING

Evolution of Digital Marketing

Marketing through Surrogates

Taking Your Brand to International Markets

EVOLUTION OF DIGITAL MARKETING

Globally, the advertising spends on the digital medium has been outpacing TV at an aggressive rate. This holds true even for India as digital ad spends are now quite substantial. This is impressive for a type of marketing that only emerged about 15 years ago.

Personally, I adapted to this medium quite early as a marketer. Let me share how marketing on this medium has evolved over the past 15 years through the lens of my experience.

Early Years of Social Media

I can say that I was perhaps among the early adopters of social media. Back in 2005, 'Orkut'—one of the first social media platforms introduced in India—was rapidly gaining popularity. I enthusiastically opened my personal Orkut account. For a bachelor like me doing his sales stint in Vijayawada, it was a great place to make new friends given that I didn't know anyone in the city. This helped me engage with potential consumers directly through an online platform. Eventually, Facebook emerged and started rewriting the rule book of consumer engagement.

In 2008, I had the opportunity to manage the portfolio of Cadbury Celebrations as a brand manager, and again, I was quick to optimize the untapped potential of social media for engaging with the consumers of the brand. I promptly created a Facebook page for Cadbury Celebrations in 2009, and set a few simple rules:

1. I am not going to spend any money promoting my page or in fan acquisition, instead I would place my Facebook page link on the last frame in my TV ads and on the back of the Celebrations pack.

2. Next, I would ensure that digital medium becomes the glue that holds all my activations together; but I still won't spend my money on it. Rather, I would continue spending only on conventional media.

So, when I ran my Rakhi campaign during Raksha Bandhan, I asked siblings to share pictures of the *shararat* (mischief) they pull on each other. And as gratification for sharing their sibling stories, I offered them professional photo shoots. I placed the pictures from these photo shoots into print advertising and hoardings.

This is how I made my existing media initiatives more exciting by tying them up seamlessly with the digital medium. And social media allowed organic growth of fans then. Through these campaigns and consumer engagement, I managed to get substantial traction for the Cadbury Celebrations Facebook page with one million following in just six months. Celebrations was among the handful of brands in India to pull this off back then.

Maturation of Social Media Marketing

> However, as all good things come to an end,
> so did the era of organic growth. Facebook
> realized that through organic growth, brands
> could achieve communication outreach for
> free and decided to put an end to it.

Today, it's extremely difficult for any brand to garner fans organically. Therefore, most media agencies today would ask you to not waste money on fan acquisition on social media and only use advertising spends to reach out to more consumers, much like a conventional media plan.

Further as consumers began spending more time online, brands realized that the digital medium can complement or even replace most conventional media elements. For example, digital ads on YouTube or Facebook can add frequency to or replace TV advertising. Banner ads play a similar role as print and outdoor. Moreover, the growth of the digital audio market through Spotify and Gaana could eventually replace radio advertising.

Like one has advertising, activations, and promotions, there can be a digital leg to any of these. To give you a flavour of important types of digital campaigns, let's probe three types of digital initiatives in great detail for now–digital films, engagement campaigns, and weekly posts or moment marketing.

Digital Films

This is the simplest extension of advertising where films can be made specifically for the digital medium. While the insight generation process may be the same, there are some simple rules to keep in mind while making films that would primarily run on YouTube or Facebook.

1. The first rule being, instead of panoramic views, digital films should focus more on close-up shots and expressions. This is because most digital views now come through the smartphones.

2. The second rule is that addition of subtitles is a must as many digital ads turn up when we are scrolling through social media on the move. These ad films would be usually playing on mute.

3. A big bold super (text) is recommended during the crucial moment of the film so that the impact is made regardless of the sound effects or music.

4. Further, if one wants a film to be primarily watched on a smartphone, a vertical camera orientation is recommended to better fit the mobile screen.

5. People have a short attention span on digital mediums and it has been shrinking at alarming rate. Hence, shorter film edits of 15-20 seconds are preferred. In fact, there has been a new addition to the marketer's dictionary — 'bumper' — or a five-second edit that tells the story in brief and can be a non-skippable advertising unit.

6. Finally, in order to cater to the increasingly shorter attention spans, the initial three-five seconds are considered extremely crucial and it is therefore

recommended to introduce the brand logo to make an impact.

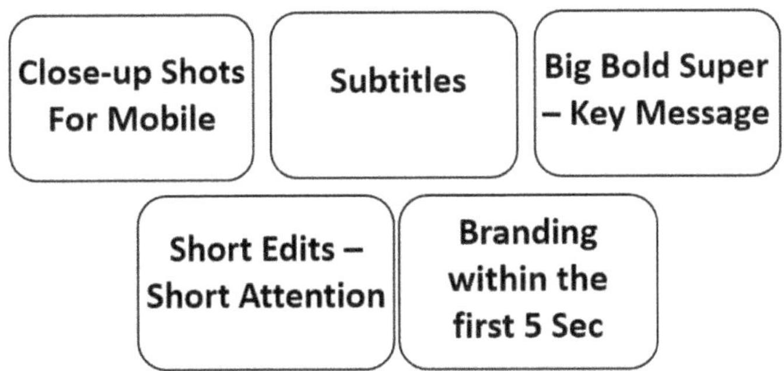

Engagement Campaigns

These are the most common campaigns run on the digital medium as they leverage the fact that one can engage consumers and provide an opportunity to interact rather than just showcase films which are considered a passive form of message communication.

In 2021, I had personally worked on Britannia Cheese StarChef campaign. It went on to be the biggest and the best digital campaign ever run by Britannia and saw metrics which were 200-250% of industry averages. Let's focus on the rules that ensure such effectiveness:

1. The first ground rule that I use across any initiative is to ensure that the cost of making assets (digital films, etc.) must always be less than 25% of the total expenditure. Essentially 75% of the money must be used in promoting the developed assets.

2. Second, while engagement campaigns like cookery shows are great as they engage the consumers on a relevant passion point, most of the money must be spent on an efficient advertising unit which is the key promotional element of the campaign.

3. While the promo promotes the campaign, it must also work as an advertisement linking your brand to the association that you wish to seal. In the case of StarChef campaign, we wanted to communicate that Britannia Cheese makes you a 'star in your kitchen'.

4. With digital platforms gaining popularity, the lines between social media influencers and Bollywood stars are gradually blurring. We managed to rope in Indian actor Saif Ali Khan as a part of the campaign for much lower advertising spend than a conventional endorsement deal might have typically cost us.

5. Digital is a topical medium and leveraging topical passion points really enhances effectiveness. Home cooking saw a resurgence during the pandemic lockdown and we capitalized on this trend through StarChef campaign.

6. Power of partnerships: Unlike conventional TV, which is dominated by specific players, digital is an evolving space. Hence, finding the right partners can often make all the difference. For us, collaborating with India Food Network (for StarChef Campaign) gave us production quality of the highest level. The channel had already budgeted for certain hours of food programming anyway and this helped manage our costs better.

Weekly Posts

Weekly posts are the bread and butter of the existence of a brand on social media. In conventional advertising, the brand simply communicates its point of view to the consumer, however, in case of weekly posts, brands need to find a way to participate in the consumer's conversation. The way brands do this is by identifying relevant topics of conversation and put out a lot of posts that may be relevant. The simplest way of doing this is through a pre-decided calendar of occasions that they celebrate, including Republic Day, New Year's Eve, Mother's Day, and so on.

However, in recent times, the emergence of 'moment marketing' has made this space quite exciting. One complementary skill demanded from digital agencies these days is social listening where topics of ongoing conversation can be retweeted or the brand can be brought in.

The key rules to keep in mind for generating memorable weekly posts are:

1. **Content buckets:** A brand needs to identify the content buckets that best express their proposition. For example, a malted food drink like Bournvita or Horlicks may wish to participate in conversations around health, parenting, and nutrition. These can therefore be three relevant content buckets for the brand.

2. **Style guide:** Given that a brand needs to be significantly more agile on social media and create content far more frequently, the alignment within an organization on a standard style guide (which includes colours, fonts,

product formats to be shown, and drool shots of the product or services) is critical.

3. **Moment marketing:** This is really where the skills of a digital marketer—to engage in conversations that interest consumers—come to the fore. Best example here would be the buzz that was created around 'Vocal for Local'. However, the trick here is to communicate in a manner that brings the brands own proposition to the fore.

Metrics of Measurement

Now, one of the ways in which the digital medium has sold itself as an effective and efficient medium is by talking about the fact that everything on the medium can be measured. However, there are a number of metrics called 'vanity metrics' that are often quoted but don't give much information. These include:

1. **Views and impressions:** Many brands boast of so many million impressions. However, unless one knows how much each impression costs, it doesn't really mean anything. Also, it's important to understand the difference between the two. Impression is when a consumer only 'sees' a thumbnail on a screen, but a 'view' gets clocked when the consumer clicks on the link.

2. **Growing follower base:** Given that most portals don't allow organic growth of followers, the number of followers, these days, are usually purchased to show the huge following. This is considered as a wasteful expenditure in recent times.

3. **Contest participants:** Again, unless measured against

total consumers who were exposed, contest participants also often don't mean much. For example, a brand may boast of having engaged 5,000 participants for a contest, however, the same campaign may have delivered an impression in millions. In that case, 5,000 contest participants do not really make much of a difference to the overall outcome.

In my experience, the only two metrics that provide an idea of the effectiveness of your campaign are 'View Through Rates' (VTR) and 'Click Through Rates' (CTR). They essentially inform you what percentage of the total audience watched your ad, how many watched the entire ad, and what percentage clicked through the link to make a sales transaction. This essentially indicates how engaging your campaign was and indicative of how effective it was.

What Next?

Digital medium is all set to grow in prominence owing to multiple factors:

1. Consumers have gotten used to the convenience of viewing the content available on OTT platforms such as Netflix or Disney Hotstar for binge watching as and when they choose. Also, the quality and variety of content on such video streaming sites today is far superior to TV.
2. Further screen times for all of us have been increasing continuously owing to the growth of smart devices like mobiles and tablets.
3. Pandemic has created a generation of children who have

gotten used to online education further increasing their comfort and familiarity with the medium.

4. More exciting advances like metaverse only promise that the digital medium will continue to dominate our business and entertainment needs.

In this regard, some of the trends that we can look forward to are:

1. Growth of smart TVs wherein a brand can be advertised through the digital medium similar to how it's done for TV commercial and hence there is a better control and efficiency on spends. This essentially means viewing ads on applications (such as YouTube) or OTT platforms (like Hotstar) which can also be watched through a Smart TV screen.

2. Rise of new platforms like Gaana and Spotify are leading to yet another evolution in the type of creative assets that agencies must learn to create.

3. Common people are increasingly becoming content creators on Instagram, TikTok, and on podcasts platforms leading to the growing prominence of influencers as a marketing opportunity.

4. Social listening is soon becoming a part of the armoury of most digital agencies to better leverage moment marketing.

5. Metaverse is likely to offer the next disruption for marketers and would cater to the evolution of completely new trends and way of storytelling.

The Marketer's Checklist

- Globally, advertising spends on the digital medium have been outpacing TV at an aggressive rate, and this has not spared even India where spends on the digital medium are now quite substantial.

- For any brand, early years of social media were about organic growth with minimal spends while tying up the various aspects of your campaign through conversations on social media.

- Further as consumers started spending more and more time in the digital space, there was a realization that digital can complement or replace most conventional media elements.

- Digital films are the simplest extension of advertising where films can be made specifically for the digital medium and certain ground rules need to be followed for effectiveness.

- Engagement campaigns leverage the fact that one can engage consumers and provide an opportunity to interact and deliver higher consumer stickiness.

- For a brand to generate engaging regular posts, a digital partner must create 'content buckets', have a clear 'style guide' and be on the watch for 'moment marketing' opportunities.

- Digital campaigns may be measured through views, impressions, followers added, and contest participation.

- Digital medium is expected to grow and upcoming trends like the metaverse, social listening, and connected television are things to watch out for.

MARKETING THROUGH SURROGATES

Alcoholic beverages are a fascinating category and, in some ways, the purest brands. Beyond the high that one feels, the reason I call alcohol brands as the 'purest' because they literally exist with only emotional benefits.

All alcohol brands that we are aware of contain only one chemical compound and that's ethanol which you and I have learnt at school as the chemical formula C_2H_5OH. Small amounts of alcohol acts as a stimulant, reduces inhibitions, and produces feelings of mild euphoria. As the dosage of alcohol increases, it causes a progressive depression of cerebral function eventually causing a person to pass out. Owning to its addictive nature and ill effects on health when consumed in large quantities, its sales are regulated. This aspect is something that alcohol has in common with cigarettes.

Now, while these substances are not banned, there are substantial controls put on its marketing and sales. Marketing of alcohol is primarily done through surrogate marketing. Let's explore the same in this article.

Why Is Surrogate Marketing Allowed?

It's easy to understand why a civil society would wish to control the consumption of addictive substances like alcohol and nicotine. These substances, if consumed in excess, can severely damage health. Also, by reducing inhibitions, consumption of alcohol in times of public unrest can even lead to violence. Yet, government does allow surrogate marketing. Why should this be?

The answer lies in the original premise that there are only two tasks for marketers: 'grow category' and 'steal share'.

> The marketing rules for such categories
> intelligently only inhibit the first task that
> is 'grow category'. Alcohol majors are free
> to try and steal share from each other as
> this doesn't impact consumption; just shifts
> business between various brands.

The Logic of the Restrictions

Now, the core principle on which alco-bev marketing is allowed is that major alcohol brands are not allowed to encourage the consumption of their products to non-users or those currently not consuming these products. Some of the fundamental directives are:

1. Above-the-line advertising cannot directly show alcohol and hence it cannot encourage consumption in those unaware of the same. However, it can make one brand

more aspirational than the other for current users of alcoholic beverages through surrogates.

2. Alco-bev brands cannot place their ads outside of bars or liquor shops as that would spread awareness of the category. However, they are allowed to spend as much money as they wish inside the bars on attractive fixtures, table mats, glassware, and so on.

3. Even online, the consumers are asked to volunteer to see if they are getting exposed to alcohol advertising through an 'age gate'. That is, the consumer must say that they are looking for the information and cannot be reached out to unless they explicitly give permission.

Hence, as they can clearly see if you are an existing user, brands can invest to build appeal for one brand versus the other. However, encouragement of category growth to non-users is not allowed and neither is promoting excessive consumption among current users.

Alcohol Conversion Pyramid vs. Consumer Products

In the case of most consumer products, there is a conversion funnel. You first build awareness through advertising or distribution. A small percentage of the consumers who become aware of a product try it, and a smaller percentage like it and repeat their purchase. Hence, the base of consumers who are aware of the brand is the highest and this narrows down to regular users.

However, the crucial difference here is that an alcohol brand is not allowed to reach out to non-users or the category through mass media. So, how do new brands seed their product?

The most powerful tool of any alco-bev marketer is called 'liquid on lips' or sampling. Hence, the conversion pyramid actually works the other way around. An alco-bev brand must first initiate trials. The consumers who enjoy the experience become their advocates and naturally support their 'word-of-mouth' advertising; this organically leads to the growth of awareness. After a set of consumers have heard about a particular alcohol brand by seeing their friends drink it or talk about it, it's only after that the mass media or surrogate advertising kicks in. For instance, if a consumer has already heard about Smirnoff Vodka, they may want to try it at an electronic dance music festival which is sponsored by Smirnoff.

> For most consumer products, in general, a marketer moves from 'awareness' to 'trials' to 'repeats'. However, in alco-bev industry, a marketer takes the consumers to trials (through sampling) and then 'word-of-mouth' to a larger set and finally spreads awareness through mass media making the best use of surrogate advertising.

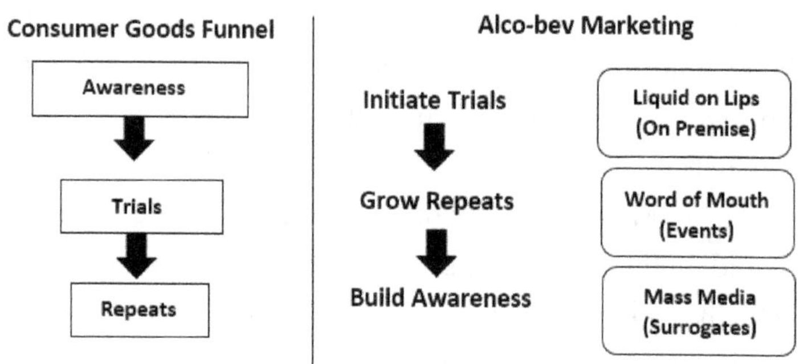

Key Tools of an Alco-Bev Marketer

An alco-bev marketer, as mentioned earlier, has limited tools in their armoury—

1. Liquid on lips
2. Word of mouth
3. Mass media of surrogates

Let's now discuss how these three tools are deployed.

1. **Liquid on lips**: These are largely offered as free samples, or, in the form of a promo in a bar. Say a 2+1 communicated through a card displayed on a table. One of the key things that brands can ensure when they do 'liquid on lips' is to educate the consumer of the brand story and offer a signature serve. The 'signature serve' for Smirnoff has been Triple-S (Smirnoff, Soda, and Sprit) to ensure that it's palatable but not too sweet. Similarly, the signature serve for Red Label has often been Johnnie & Ginger or Red Label and Ginger Ale. The objective of a 'signature serve' is to curate an interesting talk worth

consumption experience. This leads us to the second marketing tool, 'word of mouth'.

2. **Word of Mouth:** Now, a lot of alco-bev brands build word of mouth simply through an interesting story of their origin like, for instance, Johnnie Walker. However, a few other brands have an interesting bar activation kit that builds word of mouth by the creation of an epic drinking experience. Captain Morgan—one of my favorites and a brand that I had the pleasure of launching—has an extremely successful tool kit of a real actor playing the character of 'Captain Morgan' with a troupe of Morgannettes who play simple games of chance with consumers. This has led to a memorable experience.

    Such experiences are invaluable in building interesting memories of fun evenings and habits that consumers want to relive.

3. **Mass media of surrogates:** Given that the task of 'surrogate marketing' is to strengthen imagery, we see some fine consumer work where brands truly understand their cohorts. One of my favorite homegrown examples is that of Mc Dowell's whisky, which also happens to be the world's largest-selling affordable whisky.

Given the affordability of the brand, they understand that Mc Dowell's is one of the first whiskys that a value-seeking consumer might consume. Given that alcohol is usually had in the company of friends, they have hooked on to the key passion point of their target group which is a 'celebration of friendship' or *'yaari'* which they communicate very well through their surrogate of 'Mc Dowell's No. 1 Soda, No. 1 Yaari'.

Another mass alco-bev brand that has done some iconic work is Imperial Blue with their long-running advertising campaign 'Men Will Be Men'. They have created some extremely tasteful creatives around the concept that men are attracted to women in a number of hilarious situations publicized by their surrogate music CDs using music by the famous ghazal singer Jagjit Singh in the background.

Let's next understand the narrative that various segments of the alco-bev category have explored.

Alco-Bev Category Narratives

While almost all of alcohol is simply about making and packing ethanol in various ways, it has always intrigued me how various categories of alcohol have owned distinct narratives. Let's study some of these narratives that have become core to the emotional benefits that brands tend to own:

Beer: It consists of undistilled alcohol which essentially means that it's still organic and has a certain shelf life unlike most 'hard spirits'. Typically, hard spirits are devoid of organic matter owing to the process of distillation they go through which essentially destroys anything organic in them.

Further, beer is usually lighter at 5-8% of alcohol by volume versus hard spirits which need to be diluted with water to drink. As beer has lesser alcohol content, it is linked to the occasions where the amount of alcohol likely to be consumed is much less and is usually in the company of friends. It is tapping into this nature of the product and usage that beer usually leverages a narrative of friends bonding together.

Rum: It is a dark spirit and is made by distillation of fermented sugarcane juice or molasses. Given the history of rum with pirates and the Caribbean islands, the dominant narrative of rum is that of equality and of being one with the crew. Also, given the fact that rum is one of the most affordable drinks, it's also quite popular in college campuses and has overtones of nostalgia. This is also one of the reasons why many company CEOs prefer rum as it reminds them of their younger days and keeps them rooted to ground realities.

Vodka: Often marketed as the purest form of alcohol as its odourless, colourless, and tasteless and yet can be extremely premium when it comes to brands like Grey Goose and Ketel One. Given that it has no nature of its own, it's a bartender's delight and often sold as a cocktail. Its qualities of being ripe for mixing and being consumed as shots makes it an ideal party drink. It, therefore, often owns a high-energy party narrative.

Gin: It is a globally-known large category of distilled alcoholic drink that derives its flavour from botanical ingredients. However, it hasn't managed to find its space in India yet. Perhaps because the presence of botanical ingredients gives gin a gentle and sophisticated narrative, whereas in a country like India, the dominant narrative of alcohol is usually weaved around manliness.

Whisky: Whisky or Scotch is one of the most popular categories of alcohol globally. This category was pioneered in Scotland as a type of distilled alcoholic beverage made from fermented grain mash. Whisky has for long owned the narrative of a 'rite of passage' and is integral to the 'manhood' journey of a youth. Even my father introduced me to my first glass of scotch, Teacher's whisky, (when I graduated high school and was headed to college) as a rite of passage suggesting that I am now entering adulthood.

Brands like Johnnie Walker truly own this narrative as a 'marker of progress'. One subtle way this is communicated is through their different-sized bottles of various blends which suggest that as you cross milestones in your life, you show your progress by moving on to superior blends of the alcohol brand.

Marketing through Surrogates

Now that you understand dominant narratives that work magic for the various categories, let us now examine how various brands leverage these memory structures to make their brands relevant through the right surrogates.

Beer – Kingfisher

Perhaps one of the most spectacular examples of 'surrogate marketing' where the surrogate became larger than the brand itself was Kingfisher Airlines. The airline carrier was perhaps the epitome of the brand narrative—the 'King of

Good Times'. While Kingfisher Airlines may have worked well for the brand imagery of the beer, unfortunately, for the carrier itself, it was a colossal failure. In an ideal situation, however, brands should try and create the surrogates into self-sustaining business models.

Rum – Captain Morgan

While Old Monk is arguably more iconic in India, globally however, one of the brands that truly owns the narrative of comradely fun among the youth and sailors is Captain Morgan. They achieve this through large activations and events. Their surrogate vehicle is usually a Captain Morgan Cola given that their recommended serve is a 'Captain and Coke'.

Vodka – Magic Moments

Given the high-energy narrative that vodka owns, the choice of surrogates for vodka brands is usually music CDs. Here, the brands try to connect vodka to music as the passion point of their target group.

Whisky – Johnnie Walker

Given the 'progress' narrative that whisky brands in general and Johnnie Walker in particular owns, its surrogate vehicle is a knowledge series called the 'The Journey', where they cover stories of human progress.

To sum it up, the whole purpose of surrogate marketing is to ensure that manufactures do not fuel category growth or promote their products to non-users. However, they can try and steal share by building compelling brands and link them to the passion points of their target group. They do this by understanding the category narrative that their sub-categories own and then they build distinct surrogates that strengthen their brands. Often manufacturers try and build their surrogates into sustainable business models that fuel their own expenditures.

The Marketer's Checklist

- Surrogate marketing allows alcohol majors to steal share between each other without impacting the consumption of the category.
- In alco-bev marketing, the consumer first tries the product (often through sampling), then spreads the awareness through 'word of mouth' to a larger set of people. The mass media then manages to take off after a certain scale of publicity through surrogate advertising.
- The three key tools of an alco-bev marketer are: a) Liquid on lips, b) Word of mouth, and c) Mass media of surrogates.
- While running a 'liquid on lips' activation, brands often build brand stickiness through the concept of a 'signature serve', which is the best way of enjoying the drink.
- Brands can try and build 'word of mouth' through an interesting 'story of origin' or through an engagement program at the bar.

- Surrogate campaigns usually exploit the passion point of the brand's core target group to build engagement and stickiness.
- Alco-bev categories have built several narratives based on how those categories were originally produced to build an emotional connection with their audience.

TAKING YOUR BRAND TO INTERNATIONAL MARKETS

One of the most interesting questions for marketers is about managing brands across markets; this is a stint we all look forward to. I got a taste of the same as the marketing manager for Britannia's international business. In this stint, I got familiar with Britannia's brand development across the Middle East and Nepal as well as the opportunity to build a market entry strategy for Bangladesh and Egypt. Say you are working with a firm that has a strong brand equity in the Indian market with a portfolio of salty snacks or soaps, how do you go about expanding your business to international markets? What are the segments you can target, channels you should play in, media vehicles you can deploy and the role of innovation?

In this section, we shall discuss various factors that a marketer should consider while making a marketing plan for their brand as they enter international markets.

Segmentation

As the manufacturer or marketer plans an entry strategy, they can try to target four key consumer segments:

1. Indian immigrants living in the new market.
2. Immigrants with similar cultural habits and consumption patterns as Indians. This usually includes Pakistanis, Sri Lankans, Bangladeshis, and Nepalese.
3. Locals. These could be Arabs, South East Asians, or people from any other nationality depending on the market we are talking about.
4. Other English-speaking expats. These could include western expats from the U.S., Europe, or Australia.

The attractiveness in terms of low-entry barriers for Indian manufacturers is expected to begin with Indians, South Asians, locals, and western expats, in that order. For example, it's much easier to place Indian brands in a store run by Indians, and the margins needed to be paid to these store owners is much lesser than the listing costs required to be paid to mainline modern trade stores like Carrefour.

However, each of these cohorts have different triggers and barriers, and can be targeted based on the company strategy either one at a time or in parallel through distinct parts of the mix. For example, Indians may purchase a brand that is known to them owing to its familiarity, while local Arabs may prove to be an essential target group for selling locally relevant ingredients like black seed which they are aware of.

Channels

The next significant variable that impacts an entry strategy is the channels that exist in the new market. Typically, the channels that we find are:

- **Indian ethnic stores**: These typically offer low-entry barriers in terms of reasonable margins and are often easy to service given their proximity to Indian localities. Often, they would take the form of a 'Little India' like we see in Singapore.

- **Traditional trade or 'Mom-and-Pop Stores'**: These could include stores like 7-Eleven and may or may not be in a 'self-service' pattern. These stores are usually unorganized. The cost of doing business is, therefore, low with reasonable margins to be earned.

- **Modern trade**: These are usually difficult to penetrate for new brands who have with limited traction for their products, along with high listing fees and significant activation budgets.

- **Local chains**: These could include the 'wet markets' of China or Arab Cooperative chains found in Dubai which largely cater to the needs of the locals.

- **E-commerce**: This has been known for lowering entry barriers for new brands that enter the market in India. However, in the U.S. where Amazon has, in a way, monopolized the e-commerce market for a long time, listing the brand on the portal may prove to be difficult for new brands.

Media Landscape

The third important factor that manufacturers need to consider is the ease of brand building which would primarily be linked to:

- Media spillover from the Indian TV network.

- Existing media channels which can be used to specifically target Indian or other ethnicities. These could include TV, radio, print, etc.
- Cost of advertising on mainstream media outlets like the local TV network, print, radio, outdoor, and digital.

Media is, of course, unlikely to be the first step that a marketer takes. However, it has a lot of relevance while making the choice of the right market to enter.

Partners

Now, as one expands the brand's presence outside of its home market, the ease of doing business greatly arises if one is able to find partners of a similar ethnic background or favourable government policies. Hence, a few things that a person needs to scan would be:

- **Government policies:** These are often linked to manufacturing, distribution, or licensing of brand trademarks.
- **Distribution partners:** If one finds people of similar ethnicities doing business, it often leads to immediate trust as they have a similar cultural background.
- **Channel partners:** As a marketer, given that your business is going to be managed by your channel partners, finding a favourable set of partners can often make all the difference. Channel partners are usually local business houses that help distribute your stock in the local trade or list your products in supermarkets. They earn a margin of the business that they help you build.

- **Agency networks:** This is related to the cost of brand building at the local level. Agencies could mean advertising agencies, consumer research agencies, agencies for consumer promotions, etc.

Competition Landscape

> Finally, one needs to study what is going to be your source of business. As one enters a new market, the first task is to 'steal share'. Therefore, understanding the competition around you would be the key to building a winning strategy.

The key things that one must look out for are:

- **Scale and a growing market:** Now, this is not a must have, but definitely good to have in order to build a vibrant long-term business. Manufacturers prefer to enter markets like Dubai or Saudi Arabia first rather than a smaller market in the region like, say, Bahrain so you can build a business of reasonable scale first and establish an office there before venturing into smaller markets.
- **A fragmented category:** Often the most difficult markets to crack are those with one or two monopoly players as they are likely to have extremely strong investment muscle and existing consumer loyalty. However, a market with four or five players together holding half of the market makes it favourable for a new player to enter.
- **Underdeveloped market where you have a point of superiority:** Say you are the manufacturer of a premium

shampoo brand with proven cleansing benefits on the back of trademarked formulations. Finding a market with a large unorganized shampoo market or a market with a lot of low-quality competition can afford a large business pool to drive up trades from.

Business Model

Next, one needs to arrive at the right business model that one wants to build. A crucial factor to consider here would be the pricing approach. There are several price positions that a player can choose to enter from:

- **Mass pricing:** This is usually the safest approach where you benchmark yourself with a key competition and match pricing.
- **Affordable pricing:** A manufacturer here would be looking to play the volume game by undercutting the leading player by offering more value to the consumer by pricing products within 0.8x of the lead competition.
- **Premium pricing:** This pricing approach usually only works if you have a clear point of difference or functional superiority against the competition. The price position usually taken is about 1.2x of the competition.
- **Super premium:** This play is about playing the profitability game, much like Apple has played for many years in the smartphone category. However, this usually requires sizable marketing investments for brand building.

Here, an important point to consider is that pricing is usually a one-way street. Once you enter at a particular price, it's easier to go down the price ladder and make your products affordable. However, it's rarely easy to increase the price as against the competing brands without disproportionate business loss. Hence, pricing is usually the most important decision a marketer has to make.

Entry Strategy

After having scanned the market landscape, it's finally time for the rubber to hit the road and the marketer must develop a market entry plan.

The safest approach that usually makes sense is to make the following choices:

1. Target immigrants from your home market, as your residual brand equity would afford the easier route of adoption.

2. Next, start servicing Indian ethnic stores as most ethnic communities find comfort in familiarity. Ethnic stores also usually have the lowest cost of doing business.

3. Often media spillovers from the home market and some point of buying investment would be all that is required to get the initial trials started.

4. A favourable partner ecosystem would definitely help in the early years of setting up and building a new business in international markets.

5. Look at a portfolio pricing that either benchmarks your key competition or is 20% premium to your source of business.

A simple game of appropriate product quality along with regular servicing should help a manufacturer or marketer build a good entry strategy.

Expansion Strategy

After a manufacturer has taken a fair share of market with immigrants and is now hungry for the next piece of the pie, it's time to deploy the second phase of the strategy. In this phase, brands often look to target other ethnicities with similar consumer drivers.

For example, a brand of affordable cookies might find that similar products are present in other parts of the subcontinent. Therefore, South Asians are the next logical segment to target. To target such households, building relevance is important. For a marketer, therefore, running promotions inside the stores or sampling with such households is often extremely effective.

Once you plan to expand your business to ethnicities beyond the immigrants from your home country, it's also important to look at low-cost media campaigns on cost-effective mediums like digital, radio, and print to build a broader appeal for your products. Building a big consumer promotion campaign would be the best route to engage consumers and also drive business.

Localization Strategy

Once a brand attains reasonable scale and is perceived as a serious player in a new market, this gives the brand an opportunity to start looking at locals as a source of business. To accomplish this, the manufacturer would need to undertake the following actions:

1. Understand how the consumption behaviour is different amongst locals and immigrants. One will often find that product innovation is crucial at this stage. Unless a brand builds a product portfolio that is also relevant to locals, one would struggle to enter these households.

2. At this stage, a brand also finds the confidence to start listing its products in channels with a higher cost of doing business thereby taking a fair share in modern trade.

3. Once the brand is able to develop the right portfolio of locally relevant offerings and a fair share across all sales channels, one can pilot a campaign on a local TV channel and see the response to make judicious investments based on the success achieved.

Targeting western expats is usually the last port of call and usually depends upon the scale a brand is able to achieve in a market.

Entering a new market is never easy, however, the rules of marketing remain fairly consistent. It all starts with choosing the right consumer segment and then building the right Ps— product, price, place, and promotion to expand your business by taking judicious calls.

The Marketer's Checklist

- As a domestic manufacturer or marketer plans an entry into an international market, they can target: a) Indian immigrants living in the new market, b) immigrants with cultural habits similar to Indians, c) locals of the new market, and d) other western expats.

- The next decision is to select channels the manufacturer or marketer must prioritize. This would include: a) Indian ethnic stores, b) traditional trade, c) modern trade, d) local chains, and e) e-commerce.
- The media landscape has implications on the ease of brand building. We must, therefore, examine: a) media spillover from domestic market, b) local media which helps target specific cohorts, and c) local mainstream media channels.
- The manufacturer or marketer must then identify relevant partners, including: a) partners to help in dealing with the government, b) distribution partners, c) channel partners, and d) agency network.
- Finally, the manufacturer or marketer must study the competition landscape which may be: a) scale and growing market, b) fragmented market, or c) underdeveloped market where you have a point of superiority.
- All of the above factors will finally lead you to develop your business model which is often led by the pricing decision. Are you going to build: a) mass market play, b) affordable pricing model, c) premium play, or d) super premium marketing mix?
- Post these decisions, the strategy usually plays out in three stages: a) entry strategy, b) expansion strategy, and finally, c) the localization strategy.

6

ROLE OF PARTNERS

Effective Management of Projects

Role of Agencies

Partnering with Consumer Insights Team

Customer Marketing, Shopper Marketing,
and Trade Marketing

EFFECTIVE MANAGEMENT OF PROJECTS

As one takes over a brand manager's role, the first thing one realizes is that they have limited control. Unlike a sales role, where the passion of a salesperson can often deliver performance, for a marketer, on the other hand, it is inspiring others that yields performance.

Hence, the first opportunity for developing and demonstrating your leadership style arises during the interaction with the cross-functional team. What makes it even more complicated is that the cross-functional team is made of shared resources who manage responsibilities beyond just your brand.

This section explores the jobs that need to be done and how can a brand person effectively harness the potential of the cross-functional team in order to deliver winning projects.

Project Journey

The first step of effective project management is to know who you are working with and that every new project involves a number of partners. Let's now explore the journey of a typical project and understand the partners who'd help you succeed in that journey.

The consumer opportunity: Most projects are initiated by the marketing team and the typical brief is to spot a compelling, untapped consumer opportunity. The consumer opportunity could be the extension of the existing brand portfolio into a stock keeping unit (SKU) which increases access to the consumer through pricing or offers a fresh consumption experience through a change in format. It could also be a new consumer opportunity through an entry into a new occasion or a new category.

The product brief: Once a consumer opportunity is spotted, several consumer-facing concepts are explored. A concept is essentially a solution for a consumer tension. For example, a chocolate for snacking occasion could be a chocolate in bite-sized pieces in a bag or a wafer-based chocolate. Both concepts are alternative solutions for an underlying need to consumer chocolate in snacking moments.

When a couple of potential solutions emerge through this exercise, it's usually translated into a product brief and shared with the research and development team (R&D) in a particular form. The product brief, typically, has raw material and packaging material targets in order to deliver the offer at a competitive grammage and price point.

Business plan: Now, while a lot of time is spent fine-tuning the concept as well as the product brief. What really matters to the steering committee is how sound the business plan is. This includes the rationale for the sales estimate, the profit that we are targeting, the investment required to deliver scale, and the payback for the organization. The finance team is a key partner in crafting such a robust business plan.

Supply plan: Once we have a product that has crossed the research action standards, we move into the supply side of the project journey. This involves rate negotiation from the procurement team and the procurement of infrastructure for production. The R&D team bears the responsibility till the first product is produced on the line. After that, the supply chain function takes over.

Sales and customer marketing plan: After the marketing team leads the product development, an action plan is built for the market launch. This involves a launch package, distribution goals, and visibility plans to ensure the mix is driven for appropriate offtakes.

Consumer activation plan: This is the final step in the journey wherein marketing strategies are deployed to deliver awareness, trials, and offtakes.

The Stage-Gate Process

Most companies follow a structured project management approach called the 'stage-gate process', it is usually divided into five stages:
1. Idea
2. Concept
3. Full mix

4. Launch
5. Post-launch

> The 'stage-gate process' is basically driven by the right questions that need to be answered at each gate. A project is only allowed to pass through and can complete a stage if the right answers have been found by the team.

The 'idea stage' is basically when new projects are introduced. The key question to be answered here is: What's the unique consumer opportunity that has been identified? The second question to be asked is: How does this consumer opportunity fit to the organization's pre-defined strategy? And, finally: Does the idea hold the promise of making money?

In the 'concept stage', you understand the consumer and the occasion in detail and arrive at a 'unique concept' that you are trying to solve. At this stage, a 'concept test' is often done with industry benchmarks.

The third stage is the most crucial as you now create a 'full mix'—concept, product (lab sample), and pack. The same is put into a 'product concept test'. This test is quite stringent. If you get a reasonable volume estimate from the research, you can ask the organization for funds for factory, lines, etc.

Post gate 3, you get into 'launch' preparation and your factory infrastructure is installed. Here, we substantiate that the actual product meets the norms prescribed in the lab sample.

In the final 'post-launch stage', you study the business impact based on the metrics that were defined and agreed upon.

Running the Project

In the first two stages of the project, the 'idea stage' and the 'concept stage', the key functions that work together are marketing, research and development (R&D), and the finance team. These three functions can help address the crucial questions: 'What is the consumer opportunity?', 'Are there feasible solutions available to tap the same?', and 'Can the proposal make money for the organization?'.

As we enter the third stage or the 'full mix' stage, the 'supply chain' and 'procurement teams' get involved to help design the supply chain solution and optimize the profit and loss statement through the right negotiations.

Once the project clears the third stage and qualifies the research action standards, the project team starts working closely with the 'customer marketing team' to start building the market launch plan. At this stage, it's crucial to arrive at 'distribution targets' and 'sell-in plans' by the channel to ensure we deliver the launch volumes. Once the product achieves the agreed upon distribution numbers, the media plan is deployed and a rapid build-up of awareness is driven to initiate trials and start the journey of repeats and sustainable volumes.

In the post-launch phase, the project is tested through a dipstick that measures how well the product has met the agreed upon action standards of awareness, trials, and repeats.

To conclude, running a successful project requires close coordination among different teams—marketing, R&D, finance, supply chain, procurement, customer marketing, and sales—within an organization. This also offers a brand manager a crucial opportunity to build and demonstrate their leadership style and can often be the most gratifying part of a marketer's responsibilities.

The Marketer's Checklist

- Effective project management allows a brand person to effectively harness the potential of the cross-functional team to deliver winning projects.
- A project essentially moves through six stages: a) the consumer opportunity, b) the product brief, c) the business plan, d) the supply plan, e) sales and customer marketing plan, and finally, f) the consumer activation plan.
- This journey is navigated through the stage-gate process which includes the following five stages: a) idea, b) concept, c) full mix, d) launch, and e) post-launch stage.
- Running a successful project requires close coordination among different teams—marketing, R&D, finance, supply chain, procurement, customer marketing and sales—within an organization.

ROLE OF AGENCIES

The most important partner for any marketer is the agencies. We lean on them for virtually everything from building ideas for advertising, activation, to media buying or digital initiatives. But, there are several types of agencies. So, what is the right way to manage them?

There always seems to be an overlap or creative differences between a creative agency and a digital agency. During my time as a brand manager, the fights I enjoyed the most were between my two equally passionate agencies—the creative agency and the media agency.

There are also agencies that we occasionally work with. These include public relations agency, the social listening agency, media houses like The Times Group, and several other agencies that offer promotional opportunities.

However, what are the key competencies that these agencies bring to the table, what is their organizational structure, what are their deliverables, how do you evaluate their work and how do you negotiate a retainer? These are some of the interesting questions that we will explore in this section.

Organizational Structure of a Creative Agency

While most corporates are organized into
sales, marketing, media, insights, and other
functions, a creative agency has a slightly
different structure. The primary roles that
exist in a creative agency are client servicing,
planning, creative, and studio.

The client servicing team is the team who as clients we directly interact with. They are the liaison between a client and the inner workings of the agency. They take in requirements and ensure delivery is as per their client's expectations. It's a tough job to manage client's expectations and get the best work done out of the planning, creative, and studio teams.

The planning team is considered the 'brains' of the agency and these are the geniuses who help in the creation of 'concepts'. Concepts, essentially, are the link between the 'product' that the client has and the 'offer' that can be sold to the consumer. It was probably someone from the planning team of Dove who devised the connection between Dove, a soap with moisturisers, and the promise of 'real beauty' which has made it iconic.

If the planning team is the 'brains' of an agency, 'the beating heart' is probably the 'creative' team. These are the crazy folks who dream up the iconic, emotional, and memorable ads that you and I are fond of.

And finally, there is the 'studio' team that often serves as a profit centre inside the agency. As in, the studio team is central to the profits that an agency makes as the art that is generated is sold at a fee to the client directly. They work on the fancy computers and know how to play around with design, art, copywriting, and all the skills that make a creative agency truly creative.

As a client, when you share a brief with your client servicing counterpart, it's converted into a concept by the planners, then into a script by the creative team, and finally chiselled onto a storyboard with dialogues by the studio team before it comes back to you for feedback.

Emergence of the Digital Agency

Creative agencies have existed for several decades. There's an iconic American period drama series 'Mad Men' which depicted the workings of a fictionalized Ad agency from the 60s. The series presents nearly accurate ways in which the agency comes up with creative advertising campaigns, the challenges they face during that era, and so on.

Digital agencies, on the other hand, have emerged largely over the past decade. As social media platforms like Facebook, YouTube, and Instagram garnered scale, we realized that there is a need for specialized competencies that most creative agencies lack. This prompted the need for specialized creative agencies that would look after these aspects and this is how 'digital agencies' came into being.

Now, the first thing that marketers realized is that the creative units that work on the digital medium need to be made quite differently than those typically used for TV. For a creative on the digital medium to be effective, it needs to be of short duration, say 5-15 seconds, as a viewer tends to click on 'Skip Ad' the very instant they see the option. Next, those creatives should appear well on a smartphone screen just as well as they would on a laptop.

Moreover, digital agencies need a good in-house studio and content creation capabilities for superior quality production. This is because, unlike mainstream creative agencies, they need to generate a significant amount of cheap and engaging content. Digital agencies also need to be far more responsive as most brands churn out posts almost every day and expect to keep consumers engaged on their social media handles on a daily basis.

A digital agency, therefore, needs to nurture very different competencies than a mainstream creative agency.

The Media Agency

The creative agency and the digital agency create content, but that content needs to be disseminated to its consumers with optimal costs and through right partners. This is where the media agency steps in and becomes the most critical leg in almost all the campaigns.

The primary task of a media agency is to ensure that they have negotiated a large amount of media inventory at affordable rates from various media houses like television channels, radio, outdoor, print, and so on. Also, media agencies have deep relationships with other partners like online food portals, influencers, micro-communities on digital, and so on, so that they can come up with the best way to route their brand's message to its right audience.

In my past experience, owing to the sheer range of partners

that media agencies work with, they can often be surprisingly effective in cracking executable ideas that creative agencies haven't even dreamed of.

Roles of the Three Agencies

Usually, the first port of call for a marketer is the creative agency. This is because the creative agency understands the brand, its history, and its proposition the best. Their key task is to create compelling creative strategy and advertisements and are most often measured on shifting the imagery metrics of a brand, say to make it more youthful, modern, trendy, wholesome, etc., as the brief may demand. The creative agency plays an end-to-end role here. Right from the point of understanding brand's strategy, building a creative approach, to recommending the right advertising scripts, the right celebrity brand ambassador, and so on.

On the other hand, a digital agency best understands topicality. They take the baton from the creative agency and own the brand's language on social media. They are tasked with engagement or participate in conversations that the consumers are currently having. If the key task of a creative agency is to advertise, the key task of a digital agency is to ensure healthy consumer engagement through relevant social media posts say on a festival, or leverage 'moment marketing' by commenting on a trending topic. The digital agency works on pre-aligned engagement buckets and their key output is often to put out daily or weekly posts, contests, and initiate or engage in conversations with consumers.

The key value that a media agency brings on board is that

they understand media channels. They make media plans and help optimize the number and extent of consumer outreach at the most optimal cost. Based on your brand's strategy and the choice of target group, they will also offer right media elements for your brand to focus on. For example, kids in metros could be best reached through cartoon network or gaming websites, whereas consumers in small towns may be best reached through outdoor media.

Also, the media teams spend time thoroughly understanding the brand's communication task. For instance, if the brand wants to simply spread awareness of its promise, perhaps a TV plan would work best. However, if a brand wishes to deeply engage with consumers on a complicated topic, radio platform would provide better engagement. The media agency is eventually measured on efficiencies and return on investment in terms of money spent and exposure earned.

The Standard Process

The standard process usually followed by marketers is to initially work with the creative agency and share an inspired activation brief with them. As the creative agency understands the change in the consumer behaviour a brand wishes to deliver, they propose an activation approach.

This approach is next shared with the media agency. The media agency then recommends the right choice of media to focus on as well as the potential partners to work with, say *The Times of India* newspaper, or sponsorship of a popular show on mainstream television.

The digital agency usually steps in next and builds engagement as the central element of the campaign or as background elements to build deeper engagement.

While the above process appears sequential, it's actually best done when all partners get into a room and brainstorm together.

How Agencies Work Together

A creative agency best understands the brand's voice, language, and proposition, but may be unaware of the topics the consumers at large are discussing. Therefore, a creative agency might create the initial or an ideal post, which can then be further developed by the digital agency in multiple ways to engage with consumers on trending topics.

> Although a creative agency can let their imagination run wild on what they'd like to see their brand do, they are often unaware of the available media partnerships. Thus, close coordination among all three agencies is often the silver bullet that makes iconic brands tick.

Other Agencies

Often the magic element in many campaigns emerges when new and innovative agencies are introduced into the mix. A few such agencies are:

1. **PR agency:** A PR agency helps build the brand proposition into a newsworthy topic that mainstream media outlets

would be happy to publicize. They often use levers like a syndicated research to help build a story that the consumer may be interested in.

2. **Media outlets like The Times Group:** These big media houses often have large in-house teams to help brands and agencies use their full-page ads and other digital portals better.

3. **Promotion agencies:** Rapid digitalization has led to the emergence of several ways of gratifying the consumers through offers such as Paytm Cashback, redeemable vouchers, promotions through QR codes, etc. Indeed, these are the most popular ways of engaging with the consumers today.

4. **Artificial intelligence:** The agencies—that have mastered artificial intelligence as a service to further strengthen the relationship between consumers and brands—have become the new kids on the block.

5. **Hyper-local services:** Today, there are several free services like Adda App and MyGate App developed for communities and housing societies. These apps have rich consumer data and offer ways for brands to reach out to their consumers through promotions, samplings, etc., on a large scale.

Winning Examples

Following are a few campaigns I love that are a result of successful collaboration among several agencies:

1. Saffolalife's World Heart Day is a fabulous, long-running campaign. Not only is a creative and digital agency important here, but also the PR agency which brings

in the X factor by helping them conduct right studies and seed appropriate press releases so that the topic becomes more engaging for consumers than just a brand activation.

2. The COVID-19 pandemic showed us several examples where paid and 'earned' PR was deployed by brands like Lifebuoy and Dettol to not only spread the message of washing your hands and maintaining hygiene, but also bring awareness to their products like sanitizers.

3. Media teams often play a spectacular role in forging winning alliances like the sponsorships for IPL, Master Chef, big Bollywood releases, etc.

4. The Amul Girl hoarding is a great example of a mainstream creative agency possessing the skills of daily engagement that only digital agencies are known for.

5. The Dairy Milk Campaign for the 'Unity bar' with different language prints in different editions was again an example of a media agency offering the right execution for a proposition crafted by a creative agency.

6. In 2020, Cadbury Celebrations launched 'NotJustACadburyAd' Ad campaign—in collaboration with popular Indian actor Shah Rukh Khan—during Diwali. This initiative allowed the local retailers, who were economically hurt by the pandemic, to create free hyper-personalized ads for their stores along with the actor using artificial intelligence.

What's Next?

As the consumer continues to interact and socialize in new ways, opportunities for new agencies to arise and to service new requirements for brands continue to exist. A few top trends that could create the agency ecosystem of the future includes:

1. **Conversational marketing agencies:** Even as moment marketing continues to flourish, digital agencies have started to realize that even they are not fast enough in being able to respond to new topics of conversation. These skills exist with agencies which have tools for social listening. A set of agencies that would allow brands to participate in real-time conversations with the consumer is surely something worth looking forward to.

2. **Metaverse:** If metaverse indeed lives up to the hype and creates a whole new world of opportunities for brands to interact with consumers, we may, again, need new agencies that possess the skills to help brands navigate this new world of engaging possibilities or existing agencies to step-up their game.

3. **Artificial intelligence:** While we are already aware of agencies that offer rudimentary tools for brands to experiment with, this definitely appears to be a whole new frontier. An AI-powered agency could hold the potential to offer personalization at a large scale and curated experiences to consumers.

Manufacturers and marketers cannot house all capabilities within their own ecosystem. For example, in order to run a marketing campaign, a manufacturer may require help in developing creative assets for media buying, running social media campaigns, etc. While all of these tasks can also be done by hiring in-house resources, it's much cheaper to outsource these tasks to the agencies who can build viability for themselves as they carry out the same task for multiple clients.

As technology advances, the consumer demands deeper engagements and newer possibilities. These offer opportunities for the evolution of new agencies for brands to seek relevant services of. We live in an era of accelerated change and the future looks promising for further growth and evolution.

The Marketer's Checklist

- Unlike the roles in corporates that are organized into sales, marketing, media, insights, and other functions, roles in a creative agency are organized as client servicing, planning, creative, and studio.
- The client servicing team takes the key requirements from the client and delivers the same through the planning, creative, and the studio team.
- The planning team is considered as the 'brains' of the agency and they help convert the business challenge into a 'concept' or 'proposition' which can then be addressed by the creative team.
- The 'beating heart' of an agency is the creative team that comes up with breakthrough creative solutions to help solve business challenges.
- The studio team—often considered a profit centre inside the agency—holds the accountability for delivering the finished creative solution, be it a television commercial or a print ad.

- As digital portals or social networking sites like Facebook, YouTube, and Instagram garnered scale, digital agencies emerged with specific competencies to solve new creative requirements.

- Media agencies help in the dissemination of the creative content to reach consumers with optimal costs and through the right partners.

- The creative agency understands the brand, its history, and its proposition the best. Their key task is to create compelling creative strategy and advertising thereby impacting the brand metric like imagery.

- Digital agencies best understand topicality. They own the brand's language on social media. They are tasked with engagement or seeking participation in conversations that the consumers are currently having.

- While a media agency understands media channels, they make media plans and help optimize the extent of consumer outreach at optimal cost.

- The standard process is usually to leverage the creative agency to proposition and campaign. This is taken forward by the creative agency to engage consumers on social media while the media agency helps in channel selection to deliver highest impact at optimal cost.

- Given the different strengths that all agencies bring to the table, working in close collaboration and synchronization helps deliver the best results.

PARTNERING WITH CONSUMER INSIGHTS TEAM

Executing a marketing strategy without research is like driving on a bumpy road in the dark without your headlights on. I have seen several examples in which brands adopt faulty strategies and take decisions without enough data. For instance:

- A brand may be launched with a Hindi TVC Edit even though the bulk of the category exists in south Indian markets, where consumers don't speak Hindi or watch Hindi channels.
- A business strategy may be built with an entry pack at ₹10, whereas 95% of the category operates at ₹5. Such a product may struggle to find consumers.
- A new brand proposition may be launched even though your consumer may prefer to stick to your earlier one and so on.

The team that every brand manager must work closely with in order to commission the right research is, of course, consumer insights. The consumer insights team members are experts in all the tools and techniques that help answer the toughest questions that puzzle brand managers.

> However, the accountability for asking the
> 'right question' lies with the brand team.
> Unless brand managers are absolutely clear
> about what they are seeking, they are unlikely
> to make the best use of their partnership with
> the consumer insights team.

In this regard, it's critical for all brand managers to educate themselves on what can be learnt through the consumer insights team before they release a research brief. Let me now give you a broad understanding of the possibilities.

Types of Research

A brand manager can potentially ask an infinite array of questions and, hence, the number of possible research areas can also be infinite. It is therefore possible to broadly group research into two buckets:

1. Qualitative Research
2. Quantitative Research

Qualitative research is typically about questions that start with 'why' and attempts to discover descriptive insights about consumer behaviour. On the other hand, quantitative research seeks to answer the questions of 'what' or 'how many'. Such research offers more definite answers and helps in taking go or no-go decisions.

However, the sheer array of research even within these buckets is quite fascinating. So, let me now take you through some examples of the kind of questions that you can seek answers to.

Qualitative Research

I genuinely love getting to know consumers closely. Had I not been a marketer, I would have possibly run a qualitative research agency. Qualitative researchers love uncovering answers to the vaguest questions about esoteric topics like what do consumers think about a product category; they study changing consumer trends and make sense of various behavioural patterns. Qualitative researchers also use a wide variety of data to arrive at their observations from direct consumer groups, secondary research, chatter on social media, or shifts in consumption patterns.

Let me list out some types of qualitative research along with a few interesting examples that I have observed throughout my career.

Ethnographic Research

Ethnography is the branch of anthropology (the scientific study of humanity) that seeks to understand cultures and social practices of people. Unlike traditional market researchers, who ask specific and practical questions, anthropological researchers visit respondents at their homes and offices to observe their practices and listen to their perspectives.

One of the finest examples of this study—that helped build a compelling strategy for Cadbury in India—was what we called the '*Mithaas*' study. This study tried to understand how the *mithai* market has evolved in India. It not only observed and studied various famous *mithai* shops in all parts of the country, but also tried to understand the traditional and modern uses of *mithai*.

This deep understanding helped us arrive at the 'circle of *mithaas*' wherein we mapped all possible occasions where *mithai* holds a role in the life of Indian consumers. Then, we built a strategy to slowly leverage each of these occasions that could make Cadbury Dairy Milk a modern-day *mithai*. The obvious occasions were Diwali and Raksha Bandhan, which Cadbury Celebration participated in to grow its relevance. However, there were also several other commonplace occasions such as celebrating a pay day or eating a dessert after dinner. In both of these occasions, Cadbury Dairy Milk grew its relevance through the '*Aaj Pehli Tarikh Hai*' and '*Khane Ke Baad Meethe Mein Kuch Meetha Ho Jaye*' campaigns.

There were even deeper practices that were tapped, for instance, eating something sweet like curd and sugar before an important occasion such as an exam or offering it to the gods.

Focus Group Discussion

This is perhaps the most common method of conducting consumer research where a qualitative researcher interacts with a group of consumers. In this kind of research, care is usually taken to capture data from a homogeneous group of individuals, whether of the same gender, life stage, age, and socio-economic classification or if they are existing users or non-users of a product. This form of research helps to collect a significant amount of data in the least amount of time. However, care must be taken because some among the group may be outspoken and may dominate the discussion with their biased opinions.

This kind of research can help the marketer narrow down the options if she or he has to choose from a large number of concepts or stimuli. The data obtained is usually inexact, and hence, it is often a precursor to quantitative research.

In-Depth Interviews

This is usually the standard method of every brand manager where one spends around 45 minutes to an hour with a single consumer in order to get to know them closely. In the early years of their marketing journey, brand managers are advised to sharpen their consumer understanding skills through in-depth interviews. Here, again, the intention must always be to understand the attitudes, beliefs, and behaviour of consumers and not to try and use this data to make business decisions. This is because, as individuals, consumers provide varied insights. However, collectively, their responses form certain patterns that help devise marketing strategy.

I have personally found in-depth interviews to be the richest source of triggers and barriers that can lead to exciting fresh hypotheses. These can later be validated through more structured research.

Shopper Research

While as marketers we all love consumer research, there is a lot to be learnt about store placement, the impact of packaging and visibility through direct observation of shoppers in a store environment.

When marketers observe shoppers in a shopping safari,

they try and decode how they behave during their shopping mission, much like how we might observe animals hunting in an African rainforest.

Shoppers are usually impacted by store placement, as in, which categories catch their interest, how soon they can notice the category they are looking for, how the packaging helps them cut through the clutter, how the branding or product visuals entice the shopper, whether the claims or discounts push them to buy the product, and so on.

All of this can often be captured through direct observation or recording of shoppers visiting the stores.

Quantitative Research

We next come to the method of research that is most often used by manufacturers in taking crucial business decisions. Whether the decision pertains to launching a new product, packaging or advertising, quantitative research is often helpful in more upstream questions—those that need to be answered before launching a product mix. Quantitative research also helps answer questions on aspects such as segmentation of consumers, concept testing, or volumetric for new ideas.

The core of any quantitative research is to quantify a phenomenon and to understand the extent of its prevalence. The research then looks for correlations and discovers cause-and-effect relationships. Simply put, quantitative research tries to emulate the actual behaviour of consumers in real life through an appropriate sample size. The observed results are then shared in the form of statistical probability. Since we can't expose a new idea to the entire population, we should be able to gauge the differences between two scenarios and estimate the likelihood that they would be observed in real life. Also, since we can only study what we test, we need to be careful about identifying a cause-and-effect relationship. Anyhow, that's enough of technical jargon. Let me try and explain some of these points through examples.

Segmentation

One of the first few steps in marketers' pathways to understanding their consumers and devising strategies is to try divide the consumers into homogeneous groups. This then allows the marketers to take a logical call on the largest or most attractive consumer group to target.

The ideal way to carry out segmentation is to conduct a cluster analysis. A cluster analysis is done after a listing study, which can often last from three to six months. In a listing study, we get a large array of data from a significant sample size and then try and plot correlations between what we know of the target group and its buying choices. A cluster analysis essentially tries to decode what are the common factors among target groups that most correlate to specific buying choices.

One form of segmentation that I am a fan of is NeedScope—a proprietary segmentation tool offered by London-based data insights company Kantar. Traditionally, segmentation involves dividing the population according to demographic factors like age, gender, occupation, location, and education. However, NeedScope is extremely powerful as it leverages psychological factors like personality traits, lifestyle, attitudes, values, interests, and beliefs.

In the alco-bev category, this form of segmentation is especially useful as the product is often functionally the same. Most alcohol is usually just ethanol with a different colour, flavour, or taste while delivering the same function benefit. Here, NeedScope comes to the rescue. NeedScope helps highlight the fact that rum and beer are often consumed in a setting such as a group of friends sitting together to drink without inhibitions. Perhaps this explains why Budweiser commercials that talk about buddies bonding over beer are so popular. The Budweiser slogan, 'This Bud's for you' is a marketing tagline that suggests Budweiser beer is meant to be enjoyed by and shared with friends, family, and anyone you want to celebrate good times with. Vodka, on the other hand, is more often associated with high-energy settings, such as a disco or a pub. Perhaps this is the reason why vodka brands such as Smirnoff and Magic Moments sponsor key Electronic Dance Music festivals like the Sunburn Arena in Pune.

Mixed Tests – Product and Packaging

These could involve a vast variety of research and typically depend on pre-aligned action standards. This type of research helps marketers take decisions on the right product or packaging to launch.

The action standards that we typically look at are a superiority over an existing product. If a marketer wishes to launch a new product, often the action standard is to beat the existing competition in the market. If a marketer wishes to replace an existing product, then we test if it is superior to the existing product in a clutter of products already available in the market.

The most important thing that is done in such research is to build a model of how the consumer experiences the products or concepts that are being tested. In case it is a product test, 'blinding' is often carried out so that the packaging or visuals don't prejudice the consumer in favour of the brand or competition. In the case of packaging, a dummy shelf is created that replicates the clutter of various brands typically found in the market.

These are fairly standard research methods that we have seen historically to correlate with market performance.

Concept or New Idea Tests

One of the most exciting pursuits of a marketer is to uncover new ideas to offer to the consumer. The most famous methodology for testing such innovations is BASES, developed by The Nielsen Company—arguably one of the most popular quantitative market research agencies on the planet. The BASES methodology can guide the entire innovation process right from the ideation stage, where an idea screener methodology is used to filter top ideas from the rest.

Next are BASES I and BASES II; these essentially provide the volumetric that marketers can expect if they were to launch a new idea into the market.

After a marketer has shortlisted a relevant idea through the idea screener method, they can next plan for a concept test which assesses whether a concept appeals to consumers. When a concept is tested along with a product, it's called a concept product test. This tests how attractive a consumer finds a concept and gauges how well the product delivers on the promised concept.

A BASIS II, however, takes a lot more data from the marketer in terms of the distribution gain expected and marketing mix that they plan to deploy, including money to be spent on sampling, advertising on air, etc., to estimate the business gains expected.

Dipstick and Brand Tracks

Another crucial study carried out by marketers is to assess the performance of a new launch or a new campaign. This is when a dipstick study is deployed. In such a study, we typically track consumer metrics, including brand awareness, trials, and top-of-mind awareness.

It also involves taking a sample size of consumers from key centres and asking them a battery of questions that help extrapolate the effect of a newly introduced product or its advertising across a large geography. The test also uses unbranded frames from a brands communication to track if the message has been registered and the brand gets noticed.

Such research methods are crucial in making investment decisions and tracking performance against the competition.

Also, while a dipstick study measures the consumer metrics over a set duration, marketers often invest in brand tracks to monitor monthly or quarterly movements of the above parameters.

Advertising Testing

The most famous tool for advertising testing is the LINK+ ad testing methodology developed by Kantar. This tool essentially relies on a number of possible stimuli, including finished Ad film, an animatic, boardomatic, narration, etc., to study the opportunity of a new creative piece in persuading the consumer to buy a particular product or services.

Link+ testing relies on three key criteria to decide if a piece of creative is effective—ensures enjoyment, engagement, and brand linkage.

A piece of creative is usually effective if the consumer enjoys watching it and remains engaged through the entire duration of the edit. Thus, enjoyment measures what sections of the film surprised or delighted the consumer. Also, when the consumer is asked to narrate the story, we understand how long through the edit the consumer stayed engaged. However, neither enjoyment nor engagement is particularly effective if the brand doesn't play a central role in the film and this is where brand linkage comes in.

While Link+ has been found extremely effective in delivering a high return on investment, it is often criticized in being unable to decode ads that rely on culture or moment marketing.

Market Share Reports

While the methods discussed above provide data on specific consumer questions, most marketers rely on audited market share reports that track their brand's performance as against the competition. Nielsen is the largest company in this space and offers rich data beyond your own business to help you understand how you are performing among your competitors.

As mentioned earlier, the number of research studies that can be undertaken are infinite and the ones discussed above might just be a small sample of what a marketer might use in their day-to-day life. However, the crucial point to understand is: if the question you are asking starts with 'why', you possibly require qualitative research, and if your question starts with 'what' or 'how many', you are seeking quantitative research.

The Marketer's Checklist

- While the consumer insights team holds the accountability for commissioning the right research, the main challenge for a brand manager is to ask the 'right question' that can be researched. Answering this question also helps address the business challenge that brands may be facing.
- The two key types of research are qualitative research and quantitative research. Qualitative research helps the marketer understand 'why' something is happening, while quantitative research gives definite answers such as 'what' would happen if we were to deploy a specific strategy.
- Key qualitative research methods include ethnographic research, focus group discussion, in-depth interviews, and shopper understanding.
- Ethnographic research is a branch of anthropology (scientific study of humanity) that entails visiting the consumers at their homes and offices to observe their practices and listen to their perspectives.

- Key quantitative research methods include segmentation, mixed tests–packaging and product, concept or new idea tests, dipstick or brand tracks, advertising testing, and market share reports.
- Segmentation is a process of breaking consumer data into groups with relatively homogeneous behaviour that allows a marketer to choose one of the segments as their target.
- Mixed tests for product or packaging try and simulate the market conditions by offering the renovated product or packaging against the competition and studying the impact of the change through a statistically significant sample.
- The concept of new idea test helps us arrive at the business potential that a new idea holds. Depending on the stimuli available, this test becomes more refined and gives better results.
- Dipsticks and brand tracks help measure the health of a new innovation or an existing brand in terms of awareness among consumers, trials initiated so far, repeat purchases achieved, and so on.
- Advertising testing helps us arrive at the strength of a creative asset like a television ad film in creating a positive impact on the consumer. The creative asset is often tested on enjoyability, engagement, and brand linkage.
- Market share reports help track the performance of a brand in the market against the competition on various parameters, including distribution, stock weight on the shelf, and share of business.

CUSTOMER MARKETING, SHOPPER MARKETING, AND TRADE MARKETING

One of the most basic questions that many people ask is: 'What's the difference between sales and marketing?'. If I were to answer the question in the context of consumer products, the task of the sales function is essentially to ensure that products are available at arm's reach, while that of the marketing function is to enable products to move off the shelves. While sales managers focus their efforts in achieving maximum distribution, marketers focus their energies on other parts of the mix that enable offtakes from shelves. The tools of a marketer have been famously captured by Philip Kotler in the form of the 4 Ps of marketing, namely 'product', 'price', 'place', and 'promotion'.

However, there are several fields that exist at the intersection of sales and marketing. These are often called customer marketing, shopper marketing, and trade marketing. In this final section, we will discuss what these terms are, with a few examples.

Customer Marketing

Among the three fields mentioned above, perhaps the most extensive and the most strategic one is customer marketing.

Customer marketing focuses on first defining various customer types or retailers. The term most often used in this context is 'retail environment'. Once these 'retail environments' or 'REs' are defined, customer marketing proceeds to identify the needs of these channels and how best to incentivize them to deliver profitable business growth.

The most rudimentary way of defining REs is turnover. Hence, among the more traditional classifications of retail environments are supermarkets, top-end, mass retail, and wholesale. Supermarkets broadly refer to stores in a self-service format, while top-end retail environments tend to be grocers that deliver large business volumes owing to their larger stocking capacity or due to them being situated in prosperous neighbourhoods. Mass retail environments are usually the traditional small kirana stores and wholesalers or large-volume stores that essentially offer discounts and sell to smaller kirana shops.

As the science of customer marketing evolved, so did the sub-categorizations. Thus, supermarkets were further split into hypermarkets (HMs), national chains or banners (NCs), standalone supermarkets (SAMTs), and cash and carry (CnCs). Hypermarkets like Spencer's are the largest chains which have huge store sizes and are often used to create mega displays by large brands to build stature. National chains include groups like DMart, Future Retail, and Reliance Retail, which contribute to the bulk of the category. Standalone supermarkets might include stores like

Simpli Namdhari's (based in Bangalore) and other regional chains. Finally, cash and carry operators like Metro are the wholesalers of the supermarket universe.

Further, the top-end splits into high-end grocers and food stores. High-end grocers sell significant amounts of premium grocery items, while food stores might be hot destinations for food and snacking companies.

Mass retail can be split further into low-end grocers, paan stores, chemists, and cosmetic stores. Most of these stores carry a limited assortment and are of interest to those looking for specific categories. To illustrate, soap majors tend to target low-end grocers, cigarette companies target paan stores, malted food drinks are very relevant at chemist shops, and personal care would get a lot of business from cosmetic stores.

Finally, there is wholesale, which needs to be targeted with additional discounts and is critical for reaching out to outlets that may be too small, too inaccessible or not creditworthy enough for a regular distributor to offer services to.

The customer marketing function understands the needs of each of these retail environments and arrives at a scientific way of activating these stores. A few examples of the levers that customer marketing can press are:

1. **Sales strategy:** Customer marketing is the key towards defining the outlet expansion targets for a company, as also towards identifying depth expansion opportunities from the right channels through the right annual retailers and distributor programs.

2. **Must-sell SKUs (MSS):** Most companies have as many as a 100 SKUs, or stock keeping units, while a salesman gets an order of just 7-8 SKUs from a store on a weekly

visit. Hence, defining which SKUs are mission critical in terms of ensuring availability on the basis of the RE classification. This is the first way of ensuring appropriate availability for consumers. For instance, small sachets might be on the MSS list of paan outlets, while home packs might be critical to display in supermarkets.

3. **Optimizing SKUs:** The second role that customer marketing usually plays in organizations is in trimming the tail SKUs. Customer marketing also seeks to maximize distribution and reach while minimizing the number of SKUs to sell in.

4. **Sales and distributor incentive programs:** One of the crucial levers to executing a well-thought-out sales strategy is setting appropriate targets and incentives towards the achievement of the same, by calling out focus SKUs of the month, and so on.

Trade Marketing

> While customer marketing focusses on identifying channels and building a sales strategy to deliver optimal growth, the trade marketing function is more concerned with the right promotion programs that help grow these REs.

Some examples of trade programs run by manufacturers are:

1. **Schemes:** Retailers are often offered additional margins on a bulk purchase. For example, a soap major might incentivize a retailer with a 12+1 offer on purchasing

at least a dozen bars of soap. Similarly, if a company is looking to increase indirect distribution of a shampoo sachet, then offering even a 2% additional margin to wholesalers can be incredibly effective.

2. **Visibility programs:** Based on the ability of certain outlets to offer large offtakes to specific brands at specific times of the year, there is a possibility of taking shelf space. For instance, a milkshake brand would like to dominate shelf space in food outlets during summers.

3. **Cross-promotions:** It is often easy to create availability for new innovations by bundling them with lead brands. If, for instance, a new brand of chocolates is offered in a scheme along with Cadbury Dairy Milk, it is likely to be purchased by a large number of retailers.

4. **Annual tie-ups:** A few high-end grocers and wholesalers offer a large quantum of sales to a number of companies. Tying up sales targets and visibility space in these outlets is often a very powerful way of safeguarding your market share.

Shopper Marketing

> While customer marketing helps in identifying the needs of a customer and trade marketing focusses on encouraging loading of and driving offtakes, shopper marketing focusses on the needs of the shopper who is trying to navigate these mazes.

Shopper marketing understands that a shopper goes through a particular buying cycle, and that a brand can lose a potential sale at any stage of this cycle. These stages and how brands can influence them are captured below:

1. **Look:** The first thing that shoppers do when they enter a store is to look around and see what captures their attention. This is where a large and attractive fixture might capture the shopper's attention, like, let's say, a large 6-ft by 6-ft figure of an M&M's character in a duty-free store. So, the first task of a brand would be to identify the passion points of its target group, say football fans, and set up an attractive point-of-buying element.

2. **Find:** The next step for shoppers is to try and find the category of their interest. Here, dominant players in India like Cadbury might invest in creating category management planograms within the confectionary category, so that shoppers find it easier to spot the exact type of goodies they might be looking for. This is often achieved through the right 'planogram', or a layout of company products that is offered to merchandizers.

3. **Identify:** Next, shoppers go on to try and find the exact product that they are looking for. At this stage, a standout colour is extremely effective. For example, red, orange and yellow are colours that one would most often associate with baking and so they are most commonly associated with the biscuits category. In this backdrop, Oreo's blue colour helps the brand stand out and get easily spotted.

4. **Notice:** Appropriate branding, a great product shot that attracts the eye, and nutritional claims are often great elements to attract the interest of shoppers.

5. **Pick-up:** This refers to the final act of picking up a

product, paying, and exiting a store. A pack promotion or a limited-edition flavour can often be quite effective in getting shoppers to decide on buying a product.

Shopper marketing tries to understand the impact of each of these parts of the merchandizing or product-packaging mix to try and increase offtakes.

What's Next?

Growth in technology is leading to the rapid evolution of the above functions. The top trends that we have seen in recent years are:

1. **Artificial intelligence for booking orders:** P&G started the trend of offering tablets to their sales executives to book orders well over a decade ago. Over time, as the field of artificial intelligence has grown, software have helped maximize revenue by plotting correlations between similar outlets and what new SKUs can be sold. Artificial intelligence is now being used across a number of consumer product companies to drive the right sell-in.

2. **Geotagging of outlets and efficient sales calls:** Another interesting technology that has developed in recent times is geotagging outlets, so that new salespersons, who have to find outlets on the beat, can see them on Google Maps. Such technologies are also used to study the amount of time required to make a sales call that is tied to a store of a particular type.

3. **Retailer engagement groups:** An emerging area of interest is to bring retailers onto a digital platform, where

they can directly be engaged with brands launching new offers or seeking to spread awareness about schemes.

4. **Loyalty clubs:** While loyalty clubs are not a new concept, the growth of digitalization has made them even more seamless and easy to build and monitor.

5. **E-commerce:** Finally, the growth of e-commerce is leading to a whole new field of exploration through which one can better understand and influence shopper behaviour.

The Marketer's Checklist

- In the context of consumer product organizations, sales is about ensuring that products are available at arm's reach, while marketing is about enabling the products to move off the shelves.
- Customer marketing focuses on first defining various customer types or retailers, and then identifying the ways to incentivize these channels to deliver profitable business growth.
- The most rudimentary way of categorizing retail environments is by turnover. Thus, a traditional way of classification is in terms of 'supermarkets', 'top-end', 'mass retail', and 'wholesale'.
- Some of the tasks that customer marketing does, include building the sales strategy, defining must-sell SKUs by retail environment, optimizing SKUs, and building channel incentive programs.
- The trade marketing function builds the right promotion programs that help various retail environment channels

grow. The trade marketing team achieves this through schemes, visibility programs, cross-promotions, and annual tie-ups.

- The shopper marketing function helps shoppers navigate the aisles by impacting their ability to 'see' the category, scan through the SKUs, spot the product they are looking for, allow the pack to capture interest, and finally drive selection through promotions.

- Some of the future trends that we can look forward to include: a) artificial intelligence to help in booking orders, b) geotagging of outlets to increase sales efficiency, c) retailer engagement groups, d) loyalty clubs, and e) the growth of e-commerce.

AFTERWORD

Marketing is a field that fascinates many and is often seen as a 'strategic' function that leads the company into the future. However, the lack of clarity around what marketing actually does remains a subject of great debate.

While sales team delivers the business, R&D team researches and develops the product, finance team monitors the bottom line, and supply chain team ensures all products reach the consumers, one often wonders, what is the specific metric that the marketing team delivers on? This book is my attempt to answer this question and demystify the subject not from a theoretical lens, but from a practical one.

In the initial chapters, I took you through the essentials of brand strategy where we discussed the tasks of a brand manager, the role of category strategy, building a brand strategy, and finally, the brand purpose which becomes the core of your brand.

In the following chapters, we discussed the activation strategy for your brand which covers advertising, activations, buzz marketing, consumer promotions, role of celebrities, and creating a media plan to deploy your investments.

We further took a deep dive into the various types of specialized marketing, including the one that utilizes digital medium, the one that's done through surrogates, and the one where you can take your brand to international markets.

Then, we explored the crucial decisions a marketer needs to make in their mix, including decisions on pricing, packaging design, innovations, and brand architecture that would hold the brand portfolio together.

Marketing is not an island. Marketers can only achieve their brand objectives by collaborating with various partners. These include the cross-functional team through which project management is carried out, the various agencies that a marketer deals with, and also the customer, shopper, and trade marketing teams.

I hope your enjoyed reading the book and I hope it helps you in your journey as a marketer of your brands. Godspeed and good luck!

ACKNOWLEDGEMENTS

Writing a book is a labour of love, and such an endeavour can only be achieved through the love and blessings of many. First and foremost, it would be my parents who made me the person that I am today. My father, by sharing with me his occasional pearls of wisdom, and more importantly, my mother, by listening to me and teaching me how to express myself.

The original catalysts behind my writing journey and eventually the book were, of course, the crucial trio of my life: my wife and two mentors, Kalyan Challapalli and Gautam Gupta. They inspired me to make good use of my knowledge and energy to contribute to the world. My mother-in-law, with her calming presence, has also been a solid bedrock of support in this literary endeavour of mine.

I am also reminded of my sixth-grade English teacher, Mrs. Malini Poduval, who was the first person to encourage me to write. Despite my terrible handwriting, she would ask me to read out my essays to the entire class. Those early seeds of encouragement played a large role in making me the person I am today.

The book was conceived when Uday Kiran, co-founder of *Mentza* (an audio platform), asked me to share my posts with him and around the same time, Rajesh Srinivasan, my good friend, managed to glean the book out of the articles I had already written so far. I am also indebted to my mentor and guide Rohit Srivastava, Chief Strategy Officer, Contract Advertising, who urged me to reflect on my learnings and experiences in my quest towards writing my book.

Most of the early content of this book has emerged from my LinkedIn posts and articles that I wrote for marketing and advertising content-sharing platforms such as *Case Reads* (supported by Yash Thakkar and Geeta Belani), *The Strategy Story* (supported by Shikhar Goel), and *The Marketing Jack* (supported by Pranjal Pravin).

Rajesh Srinivasan and Pranjal Pravin have been my two most reliable companions throughout my writing journey. They have spent extensive time reading and rereading my drafts and have supported me despite my unreasonable demands.

I'm also grateful to my friends Harsh Pamnani, author of *Booming Brands - Inspiring Journeys Of 11 "Made In India" Brands*; Karishma Bhalla, Founder of Taramis Labs; and Sundar Kondur, Director at Bennett Coleman & Co. Ltd., who have helped me so tremendously in my literary journey.

Of course, no book on marketing can be complete until it is supported extensively by the academia of the marketing universe. I'm grateful to the various marketing professors who reviewed the manuscript at the early stages and offered their valuable insights. These include—Dr Satyanarayana Rentala, Associate Professor- Marketing, Bharathidasan Institute of Management, Tiruchirappalli; Dr Parag Amin, Registrar, ATLAS SkillTech University; Dr Rituparna Basu, Professor,

Marketing Area Chair at International Management Institute, Kolkata; Dr Surabhi Singh, Professor-Marketing, G.L Bajaj Institute of Management and Research; Dr Anjali Sane, Professor and Dean at MIT World Peace University, Pune; Dr Pawan Kumar, Professor, Mittal School of Business, Lovely Professional University; Arun Sharma, Area Chairperson and Associate Professor, School of Business Management-Narsee Monjee Institute of Management Studies; Neeraj Pandey, Professor and Associate Dean, Placements and Branding, Indian Institute of Management Mumbai; Samar Singh, Professor Indian Institute of Management Raipur; and Dr Vimal Chandra Verma, Assistant Professor at Siddharth University, Kapilvastu, Uttar Pradesh.

I am also eternally grateful to the various schools of marketing that I have been a part of, including my alma mater Indian Institute of Management Indore, and all the leaders that I learned a great deal from at Wipro Consumer Care & Lighting, Mondelez India, Diageo India, Britannia Industries, and Vodafone Idea.

The entire team at Jaico Publishing House has been a delight to work with. I am especially grateful for their rigour and diligence, which consistently gave me the confidence that my book was in safe hands. Last but not least, I owe my gratitude to my LinkedIn community of 40,000 followers for their regular engagement with my posts and constant encouragement to share my views.

GLOSSARY

1. **Brand offtakes:** These are sales from the retailer to the customer. While offtakes are not tracked by the company, offtakes trends are tracked by market research agencies like Nielsen.
2. **Sell-in:** Number of units of a product manufacturers sell to retailers.
3. **Sell-out:** Number of units of a product that is being sold out to customers (from retailers).
4. **Sell-through:** It's the same as sell out.
5. **Stock Keeping Unit (SKU):** A Stock Keeping Unit is a unit of measure in which the stocks of a material are managed. Each SKU is a distinct type of item of sale, purchase or tracking in inventory. Every SKU is unique owing to attributes like manufacturer, description, material, size, colour, packaging, and warranty terms.
6. **Data cuts:** A data cut is when available information is organized into discrete parts based on a set of rules. For example, we may choose to only study a subset of the available data at a point in time, say sales of only one particular store, or a one price point or between a fixed period of time.
7. **Artwork management:** Artwork management is the

process of organizing, storing, tracking, proofing, and approving artwork files and assets for various purposes, such as print production, digital media, marketing, branding, and packaging.

8. **Consumer proposition**: A consumer proposition or customer value proposition consists of the sum total of benefits which a vendor promises a customer will receive in return for the customer's associated payment (or other value-transfer).

9. **Modern trade**: Modern trade refers to retail sectors that are better organized; this includes supermarkets, hypermarkets, and large-format stores. These modern trade outlets are typically owned by large retail chains or corporations.

10. **Traditional trade**: Traditional trade or informal retail is a complex distribution network of micro- retailers, kiosks, hawkers, stockists, open market traders, wholesalers, and distributors. Traditional trade builds on interpersonal relations between the customers and the retailers.

11. **Above the Line (ATL) advertising campaign**: ATL is used when the focus is on mass media promotion to reach wider audience. ATL includes media such as radio, TV, print media such as newspaper, magazines, and billboards. An execution of these elements is often called a campaign.

12. **Below the Line (BTL) advertising**: In contrast to ATL, below the line advertising is directed to reach smaller and targeted audience. BTL includes marketing activities such as brochures, direct mail, flyers, sponsorships, and email campaigns.

13. **Consumer health scores**: A consumer health score is a value that indicates the long-term prospect for a consumer to drop off or, conversely, to become a high-value, repeat consumer through renewal or cross-selling or up-selling strategies.

14. **Top line and bottom line**: The top line refers to the sales or the revenues of a company which is the total income generated during a particular period. The bottom line is the net profit of the company which is extracted after all operating expenses, depreciation, interest, and taxes. The bottom line is what the company actually generates for shareholders.

15. **Category strategy**: A category strategy is a holistic approach to brand and business planning which outlines various categories a business has interest in. This approach projects the attractiveness of the segments and helps the organization build plans to compete within these segments.

16. **Purchase decision hierarchy (PDH)**: A PDH helps decode the factors that shoppers intuitively consider while making a purchase decision and the trade-offs that they make while arriving at the final selection.

17. **Functional and emotional benefits of a product**: Functional benefits are product attributes that deliver functional utility to customers, while emotional benefits are positive feelings customers associate with the brand.

18. **Discretionary product categories**: The term describes products and services that are desirable for consumers, but not essential to their daily living. In other words, rather than buying these products because they are

a necessity, they have the freedom to decide—the discretion—to purchase them, or not.

19. **Product benefit:** A product benefit is the positive outcome or value that a customer receives from using a product or service.

20. **Marketing mix:** A marketing mix includes multiple areas of focus as part of a comprehensive marketing plan. The term often refers to a common classification that began as the four Ps: product, price, placement, and promotion.

21. **Penetrative price:** Penetration pricing is a strategy used by businesses to attract customers to a new product or service by offering a lower price during the launch. The lower price helps a new product or service penetrate the market and attract customers away from competitors.

22. **Cross-selling:** Cross-selling involves selling related, supplementary products or services based on the customer's interest in, or purchase of, one of your company's products.

23. **Marketing demographics:** Markets may be segmented in several ways, including demographics, geographic, psychographics, and behaviours. Marketing demographics include characteristics such as age, geographical location, education level, occupation, income, etc., that are used to create groups and segment a market.

24. **Shopper marketing:** Shopper marketing is the use of insights-driven marketing and merchandizing initiatives to satisfy the needs of targeted shoppers, enhance the shopping experience, improve business results, and brand equity for retailers and manufacturers.

25. **Reasons to Believe (RTBs):** Reasons to believe are simple explanations for why your customers should believe you and the benefits your brand promises.

26. **Consumer immersion:** Consumer immersion is a unique method of enabling clients to spend time interacting with and asking questions to consumers in a controlled environment.

27. **Ticket size:** Ticket size measures how much customers spend per visit on an average. In categories such as cars and real estate, a customer spends a lot of money, however, in product categories such as soaps and chocolate, the average spends or ticket size is quite low.

28. **Product trial and product adoption:** The process where a consumer tries out a new brand and becomes its regular user through awareness followed by interest and evaluation. The consumer initially tries a brand for the first time; this first occasion of trying a product either through sampling or self-purchase is referred to as product trial. If the product meets consumers' expectations, consumers may then continue purchasing the product; this is called product adoption.

29. **Demographic variables:** Demographics—or more broadly, socio-demographics—statistics refer to characteristics of a population, such as age, race, ethnicity, gender, sexual orientation, income, education, and marital status.

30. **Brand activation:** Brand activation is an event, campaign, or any interaction through which a company drives customer actions. This technique aims to generate brand awareness, build lasting relationships with the target audience, and develop customer loyalty.

31. **Consumer tension:** A consumer tension is often defined as an unmet need of the consumer that a brand can fulfill. These needs can be physical or psychological. For example, a consumer may crave for a treat or experience the fear of missing out, both of which can be satisfied through the purchase of a brand or product.

32. **Need-gap analysis:** This is an approach to identifying the unmet needs of consumers, in which respondents are asked to envisage an ideal brand or product and then to rate various existing brands or products on key attributes. If no existing brand or product measures up to the ideal, a gap exists which could be filled by a new brand or product.

33. **Brand image:** A brand image is a set of perceptions that your consumers carry about your brand. These perceptions are a result of all interactions that a consumer might have from the way it tastes and feels to its advertising and how it turns up in the store.

34. **Imagery scores:** The brand image can be measured on a five-point scale by asking consumers to rate it on a set of perceptual parameters like war, friendly, bold, attractive, etc. These scores are usually compared against other brands in the same category to come to an understanding of how one brand is perceived against another.

35. **Customer stickiness:** Customer stickiness is when a customer chooses to buy a product more than once due to aspects of your value proposition, such as your product quality, convenience, pricing, engagement experience, and other transactional factors. By increasing customer stickiness, you create more value for your business.

36. **Top-of-Mind awareness:** In marketing, 'top-of-mind awareness' refers to a brand or specific product that pops up first in customers' minds when thinking of a particular industry or category. Top-of-mind awareness is defined as "the first brand that comes to mind when a customer is asked an unprompted question about a category", in the book *Marketing Metrics* by Paul W. Farris.

37. **Cut-through:** Cut-through is the ability someone or something has to get noticed and responded to by the public. This term is often used with regards to advertising. An advertising edit that gets noticed by consumers within the clutter of several ads is considered to have good cut-through.

38. **Challenger brand:** A challenger brand is a brand in an industry where it is neither the market leader nor a niche brand. Challenger brands are categorized by a mindset which sees they have business ambitions beyond conventional resources and an intent to bring change to an industry.

39. **Category and consumer codes:** These are often a set of unstated rules that many brands in a category tend to obey and those that a consumer gets familiarized towards. For example, the colour blue is often used in dairy products, while yellow is often associated with potato chips, and so on.

40. **Memory structures:** When a memory is first formed tiny connections are made between a unique combination of nerve cells in your brain. This unique connection forms a memory structure. These structures in your brain are activated every time that specific memory

is triggered—whether it's by specific colours, sounds, emotions, or sensations. If they are triggered consistently, these connections between nerve cells in your brain get 'stickier' and the memory gets stronger.

41. **Recruit innovations:** It's a term associated with a product or service innovation that propels new users to try the brand for the first time.

42. **Cannibalization in marketing:** Market cannibalization is a sales loss caused by a company's introduction of a new product that displaces one of its own older products. Market cannibalization can occur when a new product is similar to an existing product and both share the same consumer base.

43. **Disruptive innovations:** Disruptive innovations are those that create a new market and value network, or they enter at the bottom of an existing market and eventually displace already established market-leading firms, products, and alliances.

44. **Brand stretch:** Brand extension or brand stretching is a marketing strategy in which a firm marketing a product with a well-developed image uses the same brand name in a different product category. The new product is called a spin-off. Organizations use this strategy to increase and leverage brand equity.

45. **Content buckets:** Content buckets are categories of information that brands and creators use to organize their content. Each bucket is different, but they should all relate back to the overall brand message.

46. **Alco-bev Industry:** The alcoholic beverages industry or market.

47. **Conversion funnel**: A conversion funnel is a distillation of the buyer's journey. The journey begins when a visitor discovers your brand or a specific product and ends when the visitor abandons the process or "converts" into a paying customer or buyer. Each part of the journey can be measured separately to understand the effectiveness of a campaign.

48. **Media vehicles in advertising**: A media vehicle is a specific television program, digital media, newspaper, magazine, radio station, outdoor advertising location, etc., that can be employed to carry advertisements or commercials (or any other marketing communications).

49. **Media spillover**: The spillover effect refers to the impact that a TV ad has on a consumer's search behaviour, specifically their search queries related to the advertised product or brand. TV advertising can increase brand recognition, making viewers more likely to search for the product or brand online or offline.

50. **Residual brand equity**: Brand equity refers to a value premium that a company generates from a product with a recognizable name when compared to a generic equivalent.

51. **Research action standards**: An action standard defines the criteria that will be used to interpret the results or to make decisions. It is the standard that's typically used to define what is important, significant, or merits action in the report. These action standards are often agreed before the research is commissioned and the decisions that are made post the research are based on these standards.

52. **Steering committee:** A steering committee is a group of main stakeholders that decides on an organization's priorities or order of business and manages its operations in general counsel. The goal of a steering committee is to oversee and support a project from the management level.

53. **Media buying:** Media buying is the process of purchasing ad space and time on digital and offline platforms, such as websites, YouTube, radio, and TV. A media buyer is also responsible for negotiating with publishers for ad inventory, managing budgets, and optimizing ads to improve campaign performance.

54. **Profit centre:** A profit centre is a branch or division of a company that directly adds to the corporation's bottom line profitability. A profit centre is treated as a separate business with revenues accounted for on a standalone basis.

55. **Moment marketing:** Moment marketing is a marketing approach used by brands based on current trends, news, or events that they can capitalize on in order to boost brand awareness and sales.

56. **TVC Edit:** A television commercial (TVC) is a short video that is broadcast on television to promote a product, service, or brand. TVCs are typically between 15 and 60 seconds long and are designed to grab the attention of the viewer and persuade them to take some kind of action, such as making a purchase or visiting a website.

57. **Volumetric Forecasting:** It's a term which describes various marketing research methods used to create first-year new product sales forecasting. Launching a

new product or service is a risky undertaking; hence, statistical methods are employed to present a probability of the sales volumes being achieved based on a set of variables that the new product is expecting to achieve.

58. **Concept testing**: Concept testing is the process of using surveys to evaluate consumer acceptance of a new product idea prior to the introduction of a product to the market.

59. **Idea screener methodology**: Idea screening is a core part of any new product development process. It helps you to vet and evaluate potential ideas using set criteria, data (such as market research) or scoring models. For example, with new ideas you may want to assess them against relevance, constraints, budgets, value, risks, or feasibility.

60. **Animatics**: An animatic is defined as series of images played in sequence, often with a soundtrack. In essence, it's an animated storyboard. It's often used for advertising research when the actual advertising has not been created to test how that advertising will perform post execution.

61. **Boardomatic**: A boardomatic is a series of images or storyboard frames that have been edited together in a video to visualize a story. Boardomatics are generally sketched storyboard frames drawn by a storyboard artist, but also can be a series of photographs, stock footage, or 3D renders. In an animatic ad, there is movement within and between scenes. However, in a boardomatic, generally there is no movement within scenes—the only movement is moving from one still frame of a scene to

another.

62. **Category management**: Category management is a strategic process used by retailers to organize and segment products into different groups on the shelf in order to increase business efficacy and gain strategic goals.

63. **Planograms**: Planograms, also known as plano-grams, plan-o-grams, schematics, POGs or simply plans, are visual representations of a store's products or services on display. They are considered a tool for visual merchandizing.

64. **Organoleptic attributes**: Organoleptic properties are the aspects of food, water, or other substances that create an individual experience via the senses—taste, sight, smell, and touch.

65. **Physiological attributes**: These are those product attributes that are measured through the impact they have on consumers like satisfaction on swallowing, feeling of fullness, feeling of softness on hands post using the product, etc.

ABOUT THE AUTHOR

Saurabh Bajaj is the Executive Vice President, Prepaid Marketing, for Vodafone Idea since August 2022. He is an alumnus of Delhi College of Engineering and completed his PGDM (MBA) from Indian Institute of Management Indore in 2004 and has spent over 20 years in the field of sales and marketing.

Saurabh has close to two decades of rich experience in building brands through practical and hands-on methods. He has worked on some of the most loved brands in India and the world, including Cadbury Dairy Milk, Cadbury Celebrations, Gems, Britannia Good Day, Britannia Marie, Britannia Cheese, Winkin' Cow, Johnnie Walker, VAT 69, Captain Morgan, Smirnoff, Black Dog, and many more. During his decade-long journey with Mondelez India and his stint at Diageo India, he gained an understanding of what makes consumers tick and how that translates into winning marketing campaigns.

Saurabh is passionate about sharing his experiences and has given over 40 talks at various universities including the IIMs. He has collaborated on a web series titled *'Iconic Ads with Devleena and Saurabh'* with Devleena Neogi, a brand and marketing strategist and Editor-in-Chief of online marketing magazine *Icons Behind Brands*, wherein they explore stories behind iconic pieces of advertising. He also co-hosted a podcast titled *'Buland Future with Saurabh and Manas'* with Manas Barpanda, Category Head-Snacks at Britannia Industries Limited, where they talked to visionaries and explored future trends. He has also been recognized as one of the 50 Best Marketing & Communication Professionals by White Page International in 2020, as a DMA Trailblazer Rising Star CMO in 2021, and as Top 100 Digital Marketers by Adlift in 2023.

Printed in the USA
CPSIA information can be obtained
at www.ICGtesting.com
LVHW011123021124
795330LV00016B/1116